Dazzle
A Musical S

Book and lyrics by John Gardiner

Music by Andrew Parr

Samuel French - London
New York - Toronto - Hollywood

CHARACTERS

Captain Sam Galactic, the Hero
Dazzle Star, daughter of Sekurikor, the Heroine

THE CREW

Mr Speck, son of Spock, chief science officer
Alura Link, communications officer
Mohammed McToxic, starship surgeon
Pearl Pacemaker, chief nurse
Mr Suey, helmsman
Lolita Laser, armaments officer
Mr Paddy, chief engineer

THE CHORUS

Sekurikor, president of the HomeWorld people
The Wise Ones, the HomeWorld cabinet
Gary Gemini, HomeWorld disc jockey and narrator
Angela Krypton, Consolidated News reporter
Big Olga, Red Star ship commander
Little Volga, second in command
The Bolshies, Red Star roboserfs
The Sweet 'n' Sour Songsters, Chinese space waiters
Slimebag the Haemorrhage, an astral pirate
Swampey, his first mate
The Slimeys, astral sea deformities
Sue Zuki, leader of the Greasers
Rita Rough, a greaserette
Brenda Brute, a greaserette
Dave Death, a greaser
Vic Vandal, a thick greaser
Greasers and **Greaserettes**, Sue Zuki's mob
Ministar the Astronomer, keeper of the peace
Waiter at the Laserlit Luncheonette
The Laserlit Luncheonette ensemble, gypsy musicians

The action takes place on the planet HomeWorld, on board the starship "Sunburster One", on the surface of Red Star in the constellation Karl Marx, in Sam Pan's Chinese space take-way, on a black hole seashore, back in time to Sue Zuki's street corner and finally on the planet Procyon.

PRODUCTION NOTES

The set
The set for *Dazzle* consists of three distinct playing areas with no scenic changes. These are:
(a) the interior of the starship "Sunburster One" plus Transporter Tubes
(b) a central main playing area and
(c) an all purpose sci-fi functional doorway placed on the opposite side of the stage from the starship.
The musical can be played on a proscenium arch stage or on a hall floor.

The cyclorama had a silver frame attached to it (silver card) giving the impression of a large video screen. Slides were projected on to this screen, the images and symbols denoting scenic changes. The starship levels can be constructed from different size tables either lashed or battened together. This saves a great deal of expense. If slides are not used and flying facilities are available then simple, clear and amusing symbols will be just as effective.

The slides
Sets of slides are available for hire, upon application, for this complete show. They can be effectively projected from front of house by any standard slide projector. In the original performance a Hanimex Carousel la Ronde was used. Slides are *not* essential to the successful staging of this show.

Check first for availability from
Gardiner-Parr Musicals
23 Tilehouse Street, Hitchin, Herts, SG5 2DY.
Tel: 01462 457453

The jingles, sound effects and backtracks
Any company needing a high quality reproduction of the jingles for their production should apply to:

Logicom Sound and Vision
1 Portland Drive, Willen,
Milton Keynes, MK15 9JW.
Tel: 01908 663848

The sound
Principals may use radio microphones or hand microphones, these being taken from and returned to three stands placed downstage left, centre and right.

The lighting

As well as general lighting directors might find it effective to use two 2000 watt follow-spots for principals and tracking the dazzle star. Because "alien areas" require coloured lighting it is a sensible idea to hire motorized colour wheels to save on expense and the number of lamps. These will give you five holes for five different colours e.g. Bolshies' number (red), Chinese number (gold), Slimey number (green), Greasers' number (blue). They can be automatically moved on to the same colour when required or allowed to rotate, thus giving psychedelic effects to enhance the effectiveness of the dances e.g. Hawaiian number, *The Guy That Gets the Girl* number, *Space Angel* number etc. The colour wheels are made to fit standard lamps e.g. Patt 23, 123, 263 and 264s.

Directors may find cloud effects and smoke machines useful.

The starship computer

A whole variety of ideas can be used but a simple method is to incorporate two motor car flasher units in series with two relays, the relays switching the lamps on and off in a variety of sequences. The flasher units are on a 12 volt system. The lamps may then be any voltage you wish. Originally old fairy lights and small 25 watt bulbs were used behind frosted panels.

The approach

The musical can be played either by a large company or a small ensemble provided the alien principals are doubled or trebled up. Every character should be overplayed and outfront. Bantam books (Mandala Productions) publish very cheap Star Trek fotonovels. They contain 300 full colour stills which are a great help with make-up and ideas for the set.

All the numbers in the show should be moved or danced.

All the trucked furniture e.g. Dazzle's star buggy, restaurant tables, computer sphere were converted supermarket trolleys. Ask first!

The dazzle star was made from perspex, the underwater shuttle-cock from a piece of hardboard with carrying handles attached to its upstage side.

The set can either be lush or deliberately dreadful like the cardboard sets used in the early Flash Gordon series. Either will work.

Your publicity can range from give-away button badges e.g. "Let Dazzle Star be the glitter in the corner of your eye" to a hydrogen-filled star floating above your theatre. Lots of money can be raised by offering goodies like "Spaceship Lollies", "Sky-diver Crisps" or "For 50p you can kiss Dazzle Star or feel Sam Galactic's biceps after the show" or "Win a free Chinese Suey Take-away from your local restaurant".

Starship interior

Below the computer panel there should be a whole range of knobs to twiddle and buttons to press. The vision screen is merely a panel approximately 2 feet square covered with a piece of transformation gauze. Whenever the vision screen becomes active the FOH lamps dim and a light comes up behind the screen to show the face of the speaker.

The tricorder is merely a tube with a household lamp inside that can be operated by **Speck**.

Suey and **Lolita** should have a small panel to operate at the helm of the ship.

Transporter tubes

These are made of folded cardboard and then decorated. There are three small raised blocks for the crew to stand on. On hooks inside the tubes should be four communicators. These are small cigar cardboard boxes that flip open when shaken. They need to be strengthened and decorated. Look at Star Trek pictures.

Starship props and character hints

Below the computer and in front of **Alura Link**'s seat there should be a small shelf stacked with sprays, beauty lotions etc. which **Alura Link** uses throughout the show to titivate. To the right is a First Aid box with plasters and bandages preset for **Pearl** who sticks plasters on every conceivable character or even parts of the set if she feels it necessary. The plasters can also be kept on her wrist ready to be ripped off and used at speed. **Mohammed** should finish the show completely decorated with medical jetsam. **Lolita** has a range of guns and bombs hidden behind the helmsman's panel that she can produce whenever she has one of her turns. Whenever Sam speaks to her she immediately changes into a demure sweetie. **Dazzle** should sing songs straight but play up cockney and "deb" accent at the end for all it's worth. **Sam** should be plastic and incredibly conceited; **Speck** logical, **Mohammed** loose, man, **Suey** velly inscrutable, **Paddy** loony.

The sliding doors (R)

A simple system for sliding doors is shown on page x. The doors are opened manually by two stage hands using the handles shown. The speed and efficiency can be as variable as the effect required.

The space pak

Insert or staple to the inside of your programme or hand out at the entrance to the auditorium small plastic containers for the space-pak capsules. The colours mentioned in the script do not have to be adhered to and you can utilize any kind of sweet to represent the pill.

The Costumes

If you are not hiring costumes the following guidelines might be of help:

Starship crew (male)

All male costumes can be adapted from jump or track suits by simply adding silver or decorative trim and insignias. The boots can be old wellington boots painted in vivid colours to match the track suits. **Speck**'s ears can either be moulded from nose putty or a pair of rubber moulded ears may be purchased:

Starship crew (female)

All female costumes should be as "space-glam" as possible and silk, satin or cord tight trousers into leather boots can be very effective. Tops should be spacey and attractive—plenty of lurex, satin, sequins etc. Girls can spray colour on the hair and decorate the face and eyes with sequins. Matching nails and eye colour add to the effect. A brightly coloured belt should be worn.

Sekurikor and the Wise Ones

These can be dressed in full length simple drapes from liner material; silver head bands and HomeWorld badges as shown on page xi; bare feet; girls' hair up. **Sekurikor** could have a distinctive headdress and baldric or a flashy insignia.

Dazzle Star

Dazzle's costume should reflect her name. In the original production she was dressed in an all-silver catsuit with coloured boots and matching accessories.

Big Olga and the Bolshies

All the **Bolshies** wore red leotards, black tights and boots with stars attached to the red leotards. **Big Olga** had fur boots, hat and trim. To increase alien-aggro feel all the **Bolshies** wore industrial goggles and **Big Olga** a welding protective helmet with an adjustable shield. Bolshie guns were made from washing-up liquid bottles with wooden shaft handles. Silvered and decorated they can be convincing.

Chinese take-away

The chorus can be dressed in coloured T-shirts with a bogus Chinese symbol stencilled on the front. Three-quarter length pants with a coloured border to match the T-shirts made out of black liner; waist elasticated; bare feet. Chinese wigs and pigtails can be effectively achieved by using black tights as used in the Bolshies' number, over the crown of the head with trailing legs plaited behind to simulate a pigtail.

Slimebag and Swampey

Pirate costumes. **Swampey**'s hat should be huge felt and floppy. They are pantomime characters. Cheap plastic hooks can be purchased from the Theatre Zoo. Faces are green with mottled frog effect.

Slimeys

Either ragged shirts and trousers or straight basic drape to which strips of material and plastic bin liner can be stapled or attached. The ragged clothing should be filthy with paint splattered all over (greens, yellows and browns), the legs bare (girls can wear tights, men bathing costumes). The faces are covered by pulling coloured stockings over the head like bank raiders. Bin liner material can be tied into the top knot so that it drips over the face and shoulders. Hawaiian leis are optional. Slimey guns are waterpistols that should be squirted liberally into the audience.

Greasers

Any variety of greaser costume can be used, whatever is black and menacing; ideally black leather jackets, filthy singlet vests, chains, jeans, army boots and white scarves (pieces of white material are fine). The faces should be dotted with pimples before coming on the stage.

Ministar

A boffin with pebble glasses, huge rolls of paper and a Wise Ones basic drape.

The Waiter

You can use a straightforward waiter or Dr Who or Manuel from *Fawlty Towers* or even your own idea of a space-waiter. Cupid Stings were glasses with the inside rims painted in a rainbow of colours and huge straws sticking out. The straws should be glued in place; a kind of Space Knickerbocker Glory.

The Luncheonette Ensemble

If possible use live musicians who play badly any range of instruments although violin and accordion are effective. The tune was *Black Eyes* and they were dressed as nomadic gypsies with sideboards and moustaches.

The sliding door system

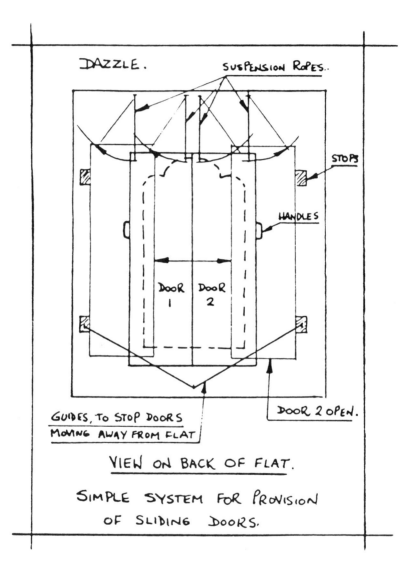

DAZZLE.

SUSPENSION ROPES.

STOPS

HANDLES

DOOR 1 DOOR 2

GUIDES, TO STOP DOORS
MOVING AWAY FROM FLAT

DOOR 2 OPEN.

VIEW ON BACK OF FLAT.

SIMPLE SYSTEM FOR PROVISION
OF SLIDING DOORS.

MUSICAL NUMBERS

Blast Off

1. Light Your Lamp — Sekurikor and the Wise Ones
2. If Dan Dare Did It — Sam Galactic and the crew
3. Dazzle Star — Dazzle Star and the Starlets
4. The Guy That Gets the Girl — Sam Galactic, Dazzle Star and crew
5. Come Ze Glorious Evolution — Big Olga, Little Volga and the Bolshies
6. Space Angel — Alura Link, Lolita Laser, Dazzle Star and Pearl Pacemaker
7. Velly Velly Tastee Too — Mr Suey and the Sweet 'n' Sour Songsters

Touch Down

8. Slimey Swampers Stomp — Slimebag the Haemorrhage, Swampey and the Slimeys
9. Honolulu Lulu — Sam, Dazzle, the Crew and the Slimeys
10. Man Above All Men — Sam Galactic and Dazzle Star
11. Greasers' Gavotte — Sue Zuki, Brenda Brute, Rita Rough, Dave Death, Vic Vandal, the Greasers and Greaserettes
12. Gotta Give a Guy a Helping Hand — Paddy, Dazzle Star and Sue Zuki
13. Comin' Back — Sam Galactic, Dazzle Star and the Crew
14. Space Angel (reprise) — The Company
15. Man Above All Men (reprise) — Principals' Curtain Call

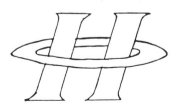

Other plays by John Gardiner and Andrew Parr
published by Samuel French Ltd

The Dracula Spectacula
Big Al
Bad Day at Black Frog Creek (with Fiz Coleman)
First Time (John Gardiner and Kirk Foster)
Mr Macaroni and the Exploding Pizza Pie (John Gardiner and Fiz Coleman)
Rocka Socka
Snatching of Horrible Harold (John Gardiner and Fiz Coleman)
Surgical Sensations at St Sennapods (John Gardiner and Fiz Coleman)

BLAST OFF

On the planet HomeWorld

Music plays for the entry of Gary Gemini. A follow spot picks up Gary Gemini, a HomeWorld disc-host. He stands at the doorway for a moment before sweeping down on to the central playing area. He is loud, hyperactive and totally insincere. There is a quiet jingly tune played behind his spiel. At the same time as he sweeps down to blow kisses to the audience he shakes hands with them, using incredibly exciting words like "Hi there", "Welcome", "Truly welcome" and "Wonderful to be here"

Angela Krypton enters. She is either trucked on at a newsdesk or a newsdesk is set for her to sit at R

Gary Hi there HomeWorld people—this *is* Gary Gemini groovin' to you up here above the clouds of HomeWorld station X95.

Angela (*surprisingly deep voice*) Hallo.

Gary Yup. Angie and Gary welcome you to another couple of relaxing lightyears with news . . .

Angela . . . views and . . .

Gary . . . music of the future.

Jingle A: Put Your Dreams On Power Drive With Homeworld X95, Gary Geminiiii!

Yup. This is Gary Gemini. Your D-5 tie-in.

Angela Coming to you through the sponsorship of Duotronic Household Goods.

Jingle B: Duotronic, The Big One

Gary It's exactly zero eight three tricorder time and we have a request here . . .

Angela . . . from all the crew aboard space ship *Interstellar Queen*.

Gary It's a space new number by top Martian group, Igneous Substrata. Know you're gonna love it! (*He gives the title of a contemporary pop title; at the time the number used was "Hit Me With Your Phaser Stick"*)

We hear a piece of radiophonic music that lasts about ten seconds with the words of the song dubbed over

Gary }
Angela } (*slowly rising together*) We like it. We like it. *We like it.*

Angela (*sitting suddenly, very serious, huge glasses on*) And now the headline news. A pathfinder survey ship was today destroyed by unidentified slime.

HomeWorld president, Sekurikor, announces the foundation of two new lunar defence stations, while HomeWorld space hero Sam Galactic receives his first starship command. That is in approximately ten hemo-ticks from now.

Gary The spacegantic event of the day. Yeah. Duotronic Household goods takes *you* live to Terran Hall for the enrolment of Captain Sam Galactic. A really nice guy with a really great future. He doesn't drink, he doesn't play around——

Angela And he makes all his own clothes.

Gary Angie, take it away ...

The Lights fade as Gary Gemini exits L

The spot centres on Angela

Jingle D: Space News Coming To You Live From Station X95—Duotronic Household Goods

Angela Angela Krypton. Consolidated News. Reporting live. Deep, deep in the deep recesses of Terran Hall. Sixteen megablocks below the surface of HomeWorld. You can almost touch the sense of awe and expectancy as the Wise Ones, led by our beloved President Sekurikor, take up their places of Wisdom.

Sekurikor enters through the slide doors R *and the Wise Ones file into group placings over the entire set. The Lights change to gold. They are singing the chorus as they enter*

Song 1: Light Your Lamp

Wise Ones	Seek and ye shall find
	Strive and you will climb
	Search and win the prize of life now
	Light your lamp
	Light your lamp
	Let it shine
	Fly above the night
	Blind the evil light
	Fight and break the chains of time now
	Light your lamp
	Light your lamp
	Let it shine
Sekurikor	When children ask the question
	Where does the water kiss the shore?
	Or why the whispering winds of time
	Can change into a roar?
	When wise men ask why heavens weep
	Yet the flowers laugh and bloom?
	Why lovers' eyes can speak such lies
	But a mirror tell the truth
	I answer

Wise Ones	Seek and ye shall find
	Strive and you will climb
	Search and win the prize of life now
	Light your lamp
	Light your lamp
	Let it shine
	Fly above the night
	Blind the evil light
	Fight and break the chains of time now
	Light your lamp light your lamp
	Let it shine
Sekurikor	For causes, there are reasons
	Though they cannot be defined
	For questions there are answers
	If you will take the time
	So light your lamp and let it shine
	Smooth the wrinkled brow of night
	Open wide the gates of wisdom
	And flood your life with light
	So you can
Wise Ones	Seek and ye shall find
	Strive and you will climb
	Search and win the prize of life now
	Light your lamp
	Light your lamp
	Let it shine
	Fly above the night
	Blind the evil light
	Fight and break the chains of time now
	Light your lamp, light your lamp,
	Light your lamp
	Let it shine

Angela And as the strains of the HomeWorld Space Psalm fade upwards, mingling with the beautiful old beams of the early Thatcher, late Wimpey architecture, Sekurikor speaks.

Sekurikor HomeWorld people.

Sudden fast and loud burst of applause which he silences with a swift gesture

We have met here today to do honour to space hero Sam Galactic and his Star Blade squadron.

Applause—silenced

Bring him before us and let the names be named.

Music processional (E). The Wise Ones clap in time with the music as Sekurikor steps down from the door R. *The clapping stops as . . .*

Suddenly Sam Galactic appears at the door of the starship L. *A follow spot lights him*

As each crew member is named, Angela Krypton floats towards them and takes a flash photograph for the Consolidated News scrapbook. After each speaks, he or she moves to a set position C

Sam (*as he enters*) Sam Galactic. Hero. Handsome.

He poses, freezes as his photo is taken

Make-up—Duotronic Household Goods.

Speck enters at the slide doors R

Speck Mr Speck. Son of Spock . . . and Mrs Spock.

Freeze, pose, flash

Chief science officer. (*He holds up a kiddies' chemistry set*)

Alura enters DL

Alura Alura Link. (*She chews*) Trained at the Beauty and Charm Aerospace Center, California.

Freeze, pose, flash

Get the message? (*She winks at the audience*)

Mohammed enters DR

Mohammed Mohammed McToxic. Chief surgeon.

Freeze, pose, flash

(*Producing a huge saw*) I am the greatest.

Pearl enters at the Sunburster door

Pearl Pearl Pacemaker. Chief nurse.

Freeze, pose, flash

(*Producing a little medical case with a red cross inscribed "First Aid"*) I am the kindest, gentlest, tenderest and, by the grace of God, so full of all the milk of human kindness, that I am (*she pauses*) pitiful.

Suey enters by the slide door R

Suey Mr Suey. Chief helmsman. Train at Chow Mein University.

Freeze, pose, flash

(*Producing a book entitled "Tips on Take-aways"*) Black belt for flower arrangement. Ha! (*He karate chops the book and hurts himself. He crosses C*)

Pearl meets him and sticks a big piece of plaster on the injured hand

Lolita enters DR

Lolita Lolita Laser. Armaments. (*She carries a huge automatic space weapon*)

Freeze, pose, flash

You load 'em! I fire 'em!

We hear a terrible racket like buckets being kicked and a scream as Paddy enters at the Sunburster door L

Paddy Mr Paddy. Chief engineer.

Freeze, pose, flash

(*Producing a huge box marked "Irish Lego"*) Trained for tirty years at Black and O'Decker's space academy, County Cork. Failed.

The chorus vocalize disappointment as Paddy joins the rest of the crew C

Angela (*to the audience*) The investiture is about to commence.
Sekurikor (*mounting steps* R) Kneel Sam.

The crew turn and kneel facing Sekurikor

Angela Sam is kneeling.
Sekurikor In the star year three-two-seven-two the HomeWorld Federation is proud to invest you with your B.Sc.

The Wise Ones place the object before him and Sam touches same to denote acceptance

Angela Big shiny certificate.
Sekurikor Your D.W.D.W.
Angela Dr Who Digital Watch.
Sekurikor And your C.S.W.V.
Angela Complete Set of Warm Vests.
Sekurikor We shall now dub you.
Angela Sam is being dubbined.
Sekurikor We shall now dub you Space Commander and entrust the starship Sunburster One to your care.

The Wise Ones pick up the tune and hum

Go forth immediately and pack up all your belongings in your old space bag and smile, smile, smile. What's the use of worrying, it never was worthwhile. So. Pack up your troubles in your old space bag and smile ... smile ... smile ...
Sam (*suddenly leaping up to face front*) My crew is prepared.

They leap up

Sekurikor Prepared for anything?
Sam Everything!
Sekurikor Even?
Sam Not?
Angela No.
Sekurikor Yes. Even Mission Impossible?
Sam Certainly. I am Sam Galactic. (*Rim shot*)

Alura Hero of the Andromedan Wars. (*Rim shot*)
Speck Nurtured on Kentucky Fried Chicken. (*Rim shot*)
Lolita (*like a wild cat*) Muscles tuned like piano wire. (*Rim shot*)
Mohammed (*with Ali shuffle*) Purrs like a pussycat—punches like a poof.
(*Rim shot*)
Pearl (*stars in her eyes*) Sublime. (*Rim shot*)
Suey Substantial! (*Rim shot*)
Paddy Subnormal! (*Rim shot*)
Sam I have never allowed Blake's Seven-Up to pass my lips. I am capable of
all things. I am the original. The unique——
Sekurikor Space bore.

As Sam speaks the Wise Ones and Sekurikor fade from the set

The Light narrows on to the crew

Sam I-am-too-good-to-be-true.
Angela He really is *very* good.
Sam (*to the crew*) Do we fear the Mission "Impossible"? (*He says "Impos-*
sible" in a phoney French accent)
Angela Sam is also bi-lingual.
Crew No!
Sam No! For if Dan Dare did it—then we can do it too!

The crew move into positions on the central playing area for song and dance

Song 2: If Dan Dare Did It

(*Singing*)	To every man there comes a time
	When decisions are decisioned
	When a crack space team has to be picked
	As precisely as precision
	A Wonder Woman, a Captain Storm
	Incredible Hulks with brain and brawn
	Who'll fight for right
	From dusk till dawn
	In my Sunburst Star division
Sam ⎱	'Cos if Dan Dare did it
Crew ⎰	I bet that we can do it too
	Yeah if Dan Dare did it
	I bet that we can do it too
	Sweet space dollies
	With eyes of blue
	Look like angels
	But do kung fu
	Yeah if Dan Dare did it
	I bet that we can do it too
Lolita	If Dan Dare did it
Pearl	We bet that we can do it too
Alura	We're space age beauties

	Got our phasers trained on you
	Alura Link and Pretty Pearl
	Lolita L the hot shot girl
Sam }	Yeah if Dan Dare did it
Crew }	We bet that we can do it too
Girls	We've gotta lotta space to fly
Men	Gotta lotta stars to see
Girls	Gotta lotta big bad guys to zap
All	On this starship odyssey-ey-ey
Sam }	Yeah if Dan Dare did it
Crew }	We bet that we can do it too
Mohammed	If you need a surgeon
	I'm the very man for you
	I fix false hands
	And screw on thumbs
	Even made some bionic bums
Sam }	Yeah if Dan Dare did it
Crew }	I bet that we can do it too
	Yeah if Dan Dare did it
	I bet that we can do it too
	If you need adventure
	We're the very crew for you
	We're Superman
	And mighty Thor
	Two thousand and one
	And a little bit more
	Yeah if Dan Dare did it
	I bet that we can do it
	If Dan Dare did it
	I bet that we can do it
	If Dan Dare did it
	I bet that we can do it
	If Dan Dare did it
	I bet that we can do it too
	Pow

At the end of the dance, over the applause Gary Gemini enters by the slide doors R

Gary (*ingratiatingly*) Great kids.

The crew stride across on to the spaceship interior as it lights

There they go. Sam Galactic and his newly appointed crew preparing for their latest mission and remember, HomeWorld people——

There is a note and the crew freeze in mid-action

——all starship personnel are supplied with Nova Star Choc Bars——

The crew whip one out

—from Duotronic Household Goods.

*Jingle F: When you're flying near or far nibble away at Nova Star Duotronic!!
The big one*

   Gary exits

*The crew come out of freeze and take a huge mimed bite out of choc bars; as
Sam hears the Star Trek music signal he is about to speak but he needs to
swallow choc before clarity is observed—now he can be taken seriously*

Sam Captain's log ... star date 3272 point one ... (*Gesturing to the
   audience*) You are about to witness the voyage of starship Sunburster One
   ... its two-act mission, including interval ... to explore strange worlds ...
   to seek out new life and new civilizations ... to boldly go where no space-
   bore has gone before.

Alura (*spraying her hair*) Assuming standard orbit around planet Home-
   World, Captain.

Sam Steady as she sprays, Alura.

Paddy I'll check the main energy tubes, sir.

Sam Check Mr Paddy.

   Paddy exits through the starship door

   Mr Suey.

Suey Orbit course velly secure, Claptain.

Sam Maintain that course. Bones. (*He starts to beat out a bongo rhythm*)

*Mohammed turns from the computer area and reggaes down to the Captain.
He sings "Dem bones dem bones dem dry bones"*

Mohammed (*arriving*) When Sam starts drummin' then I come runnin'.

Sam Dr McToxic—ensure that all Elastoplast sick bays are fully functional.

Mohammed When Sam speaks the word, I fly like a bird.

Sam Miss Pacemaker will assist you.

Pearl (*purring*) In every possible way.

Mohammed There is a pain. (*Mock agony, hand to head*) In my brain.

Pearl (*every ready*) No disaster, here's a plaster. (*She sticks an Elastoplast
   strip above his right eye*)

Mohammed I like it.

   Paddy bursts in as they exit through the starship door

Paddy Captain. Captain. One of the energy panels is badly damaged.

Sam How badly?

Paddy Well sir, the glass is broken on both sides, sir.

Sam Fix it.

Paddy Yes sir ... but *I'll* need some help, also, as well.

Sam Lolita.

Lolita (*leaping up like a wild cat, brandishing her gun*) I'll kill 'em, disin-
   tegrate their eyeballs. Let me at them. (*She is a space Annie Oakley*)

Sam Lolita.

She freezes

Assist Paddy in the engine room.
Lolita (*completely calm*) Certainly Captain, it'll be a pleasure.
Paddy And it'll be a pleasure working with you again, Lolita.
Sam Have you worked with her before?
Lolita (*archly*) No Captain, but he's thought about it before.

They both exit through the door

Speck (*looking down the tricorder*) Sensors registering some form of energy, Captain.
Sam Spot it Speck and speak.
Speck Its probes are making a logical shape, sir.
Sam Lock on probes, helmsman.
Suey Plobe locking, velly soon, Captain.
Alura (*doing her eyelashes*) Some kind of life force, sir.
Speck Communication channel open.
Sam Audio-visual, Mr Suey.
Suey Audio-visual on.

We hear a humming sound. The Lights fade and a light behind vision screen comes up

Mohammed enters with Pearl

Mohammed When that screen starts hummin', then somethin's comin'.

Sekurikor appears behind the screen

Pearl (*spotting the face of Sekurikor on the screen*) Holy Codeine! It's President Sekurikor.
Sekurikor Galactic?
Sam President?
Sekurikor Your mission.
Sam Speak.
Sekurikor To safely deliver my one and only daughter . . .
Crew (*breathlessly, out to the audience*) Dazzle Star!
Sekurikor Dazzle Star—to safely deliver her to her finishing school on Procyon (*to rhyme with "Orion"*) in the constellation of Canis Minor.
Sam What will she be finishing there, O wisest one?
Sekurikor I'll tell you when she's finished.
Speck That is logical, Captain.
Sam Very well it shall be done. Scanner off.

The Light fades on the vision screen and comes up on the starship interior

Sekurikor exits

Suey Lodger and out. (*Roger and out*)
Sam New course. Warp factor five.
Alura (*dabbing scent behind her ear*) Channel number five, Captain.
Sam Navigation?

Paddy (*off*) Hearing you loud and o'leary, sir.
Sam Report to the bridge as soon as all energy wells are completed.
Paddy (*off*) Right you are, sir.

A champagne cork pops off-stage. Lolita giggles. Sam is not amused

Sam (*back to business*) Miss Link . . . take this down.
Alura (*taking it the wrong way but enthusiastic*) Pardon, sir?
Sam Record this data.
Alura (*disappointed, producing a secretarial pad*) Oh. Yes sir.
Sam Captain's log . . . stardate three-two-seven-two point two . . . on course
for the planet Procyon. Scheduled task? To keep matter scanners on alert
for small asteroid carrying President Sekurikor's daughter, Dazzle Star,
towards our starship for link up.
Alura (*adoringly—out front*) You know you can't help admiring Sam
Galactic.
Sam (*sharply*) And if you don't, you don't work here any more.
Pearl Scanner feelies making contact with unidentified object, sir.
Mohammed Must be Dazzle Star.
Alura (*very excited like a schoolgirl*) Oh Sam, Sam. You promised that I
could activate the space searchlight probe next time.
Sam No. I've decided that it's Mr Speck's turn.

Alura pokes out her tongue at Speck

Speck (*smugly*) Thank you, Captain. There should be precedents in nature.

Paddy enters through the slide doors, looking worn out

Paddy Energy wells fixed, sir.

Lolita follows him on

Lolita I think he ought to sit down, Captain.
Paddy (*slumping into his seat*) Sure I'm exhausted.
Pearl A spoonful of SpaceNatogen, Paddy. (*She pours a prepared spoonful
down*)
Paddy God bless you.
Mohammed He should give up half the work he does, Captain.
Sam (*out front—it's one of his awful jokes*) Which half should he give up,
Bones? Talking about it or thinkin' about it? (*He clicks his fingers as a
signal to laugh*)
Crew (*in unison with huge grins*) Ha. Ha. Ha. (*The grins immediately change
back into bored sneers as they swivel back to the operation panels*)
Suey Tlactor beams picking up asteloid velly clear.
Alura (*doing her face*) Compact Powder strong.
Pearl Shuttle Star leaving asteroid, sir.
Sam Stabilize starship at zero.
Lolita Stabilizing at zero.
Speck All non-essentials at standby.
Alura Look, Captain, here she comes.

The Lights fade slightly on the starship

Pearl (*handing Sam a silly telescope*) Non-strain viewscope, Captain.
Sam (*taking it*) Searchlight probe on.

A follow spot picks up Dazzle who is either trucked or lowered or flown on

Lolita (*spinning her space gun*) Great balls of fire.
Paddy Sure 'tis a miracle.
Mohammed Well hush ma mouth and call me Joe Frazier.
Sam (*impressed by what he sees; slowly closing the telescope*) Beam her aboard, Mr Speck.
Speck Accurately but without emotion, sir.

The follow spot tracks Dazzle's entrance. She is chaperoned by two Starlets who dance and accompany her in the song

Song 3: Dazzle Star

Dazzle
If one night you stare
Through the freezing pearled air
Beyond the silver moons of Hydra
Past Orion's bloodstained hair
You will see me
Yeah yeah.
You will see me
The bright one
Dazzle Star.

I'm Dazzle Star
Child of the sky
I'm Dazzle Star
Born to fly
I'm Dazzle Star
Pretty Dazzle Star
I'll be the glitter
In the corner of your eye

If you search the icy thresholds
Of Andromeda and Mars
To where sweet Venus rides Auriga
And Sagitta shoots the stars
You will find me
Yeah yeah
You will find me
The bright one
Dazzle Star

Dazzle
Starlets
Crew
I'm Dazzle Star
Child of the sky
I'm Dazzle Star
Born to fly
I'm Dazzle Star

> Pretty Dazzle Star
> I'll be glitter
> In the corner of your eye

The last chorus is reprised

Sam (*sweeping down on to the main playing area to meet her*) Tell me Miss Star were you really turbo-lifted here from the misty skies?

Dazzle No. HomeWorld airport. (*She has a cockney accent*)

Sam (*tightlipped to the audience*) I think it's going to be one of those days.

Dazzle (*as if she has just learned the line*) Take me to your leader.

Sam I am the leader! (*To the audience*) See what I mean?

Sam takes Dazzle by the hand and leads her on to the starship interior and the Lights come up on the starship

Speck Orbit clearance made, Captain.

Suey Destination?

Dazzle The planet Procyon.

Sam You are very well informed, Miss Star.

Dazzle (*out front; vacant*)Yeah I am ain't I?

Sam (*suddenly*) To your posts!

They all jump around and run to their chairs etc. hardly moving anywhere

Mohammed When Sam says sumthin'
　　　　　We all start jumpin'.

Dazzle Excitin' innit? (*To Speck*) Jist like goin' on 'oliday.

Speck I find your simile superficial, if you will excuse me.

Dazzle Ooo-er.

Sam Mr Paddy, check the fixed transistor.

Paddy It's all right sir. I've made a portable.

Sam A portable what?

Paddy I don't know yet sir. I've only made the handle.

He produces it and exits

Dazzle Bit of a loony in'e?

Lolita No he was educated beyond his intelligence.

Pearl He will need a sedative.

Pearl exits with her first aid bag

Suey Villibility velly clear, Captain.

Dazzle Cor look at those stars.

The Light narrows or a follow spot on Sam and Dazzle

Sam Your first time in space ... Dazzle? (*He looks in at her*)

Dazzle Yeah ... first time ... (*she looks in at him*) ... Sam.

They both look out front together and during the next piece of duologue Dazzle's should come out at tremendous speed

Sam Dazzle.

Dazzle Wot?
Sam (*after a pause*) I think . . . I should warn you.
Dazzle Warn me?
Sam Yes. (*After a pause*) All women find me—
Dazzle Wot?
Sam Totally irresistible.
Dazzle Ooo-er.
Sam (*after a pause*) Whatever happens—
Dazzle Yeah?
Sam (*after a pause*) Don't fall in love with me.
Dazzle Do people do that?
Sam Yes. Even my mother fell in love at first sight.
Dazzle Did she?
Sam Of course.
Dazzle Why?
Sam Why?
Dazzle Why?
Sam Why? Because I'm *too* good looking.
Dazzle I don't mind.
Sam You don't?
Dazzle No. Jist as long as I can rely on you after the show.
Sam I am totally reliable.
Dazzle (*to the audience*) In'e luvly?
Sam I am the kind of space-bore who always gets the girl in the end.
Dazzle (*sensing danger*) 'Ere you ain't gonna sing a song are ya?

Paddy and Pearl poke their noses round the door and join the dance

Sam Affirmative.
Crew (*out front*) Ooo-er.

They descend on cue music to dance and sing the number on the central playing area

Song 4: The Guy That Gets the Girl

Sam }
Crew }
In every movie
There's someone groovy
The guy that gets
The girl in the end
He's really funky
Big and chunky
The guy that gets
The girl in the end.
He makes you feel defenceless
Stupified and senseless
He's a milk-choc whipple
A raspberry ripple
The guy that gets
The girl in the end.

Girls	Watch him
	At the space flicks
	Flex his radio-actives.
	Chasing astral pirates
	Through the air.
	Leaping
	Over rainbows
	Like a
	Martian Brando
Full Crew	Saving all those sweeties
	In distress. OOO!
Sam } **Crew** }	In every movie
	There's someone groovy
	The guy that gets
	The girl in the end
	He's really funky
	Big and chunky
	The guy that gets
	The girl in the end
	He makes you feel defenceless
	Stupefied and senseless
	He's a milk-choc whipple
	A raspberry ripple
	The guy that gets
	The girl in the end.
Girls	See him
	In the jungle
	Flex his
	Tarzan muscles
	Swingin' through the trees
	With Boy and Jane.
	Shootin'
	Silver six guns
	At those
	Injun wigwums
Full Crew	Cutting all those big chiefs
	Down to size. Ug!
Sam } **Crew** }	In every movie
	There's someone groovy
	The guy that gets
	The girl in the end
	He's really funky
	Big and chunky
	The guy that gets
	The girl in the end.
	Oh so sweet and chewy
	Make you go all gooey
	He's a finger lickin'

Cuddly chicken
Milk-chock whipple
Raspberry ripple
Guy that gets the girl
Guy that gets the girl
Guy that gets the girl
In
The end!

During applause they take up positions in the ship

Suey Claptain. Deflector shields just snapped on, auro- aumo- ... by themselves.

Speck Indications of energy turbulence.

Mohammed Big trouble.

Alura I can feel its sensor probes, sir.

Dazzle Ay ay sunnink's up!

Lolita Red Shadow coming sir. I'll pulverize it. (*She whips out a blaster*)

Speck Hold present course.

Lolita (*cooling*) Yes sir.

Sam Diminish to warp factor one.

Paddy (*confused*) What does that mean, sir?

Sam I don't know. It's in the script.

Dazzle (*to the audience*) You can see why the birds fall for 'im can't yer?

Suey Calculations would suggest Red Star.

Sam (*showing off*) Nova Rouge?

Speck Yes sir. We are being probed by a Red Star ship.

Sam Identify.

Lolita Red Star ship Bolshevik Two.

Alura From the constellation Karl Marx.

Pearl You don't mean?

Mohammed Yea. Red Star at night, Comrades' delight.

Paddy I can see a burning red glow, sir.

Dazzle (*to the audience*) It's a satellite.

Sam Exactly.

Pearl It must be the Bolshies, sir.

Dazzle Bolshies! Blimey what are they like?

Alura Hideous.

Lolita Evil.

Mohammed Foreigners.

Dazzle Ooo-er.

Speck Red Star Bolshies have hairy bodies and ravish all that cross their path.

Dazzle No!

Speck Yes and the men are almost as bad.

Alura Bolshevik Two locking on to us sir.

Lolita Encircled by kryptonic grappling beams.

Dazzle What?

Lolita The KGBs.

Dazzle Nasty.
Mohammed Hold on everybody.

The starship jolts. Lights up and down. The crew stagger

Pearl Video screen activating, sir.

The screen lights up to show Big Olga, leader of the Bolshies

Sam Identify yourself.
Big Olga I am Big Olga, Kommandant of ze Red Star ship Bolshevik Two.
Sam A privilege for you to meet me.
Big Olga You haf stupidly trespassed into Red Star territory and worse, you haf interrupted my veight-liftink class! Because of zis stupidity I haf drained your starship of all power!
Speck So?
Big Olga So you vill continue in orbit vile you and three off your comrades report to our star surface. Ve are very angry. Oi!

The screen goes blank. Olga exits

Sam Mr Suey?
Suey (*confirming*) Source power is very weak sir.
Sam Mr Paddy, can you compensate for this loss of energy?
Paddy Well, sir, I once saw a Martian mystic create incredible energy by holding his breath for nearly two hours.
Sam How did he do this?
Paddy I don't know sir. He died before he could tell us.
Alura Five points lost on energy reserve, Captain.
Sam Captain's log star date 3272 point 3. Starship Sunburster One en route for Procyon has been placed under surveillance by the Red Star ship Bolshevik Two. I have decided that myself and three starship personnel will beam down to the Red Star surface. I shall also place in the transporter room, the girl——

Dazzle looks at him and makes twitchy kissing sounds

—er—the woman, Dazzle Star. This is purely a safety precaution.
Dazzle (*to the audience*) In'e smashin'?

Speck takes her to one side as the crew prepare instruments

Speck Miss Dazzle, I would remind you that beauty is purely transitory.
Dazzle Is it?
Speck Certainly. Nevertheless the Captain does possess certain emotional forces unknown to Vulcans, that can be directed at the hearts of specific humans. I believe that this is often referred to as (*he can hardly bear to say the word*) "love"——

The crew stiffen

—and although totally illogical it can at times, inexplicably, penetrate the heart of the HomeWorld female.
Dazzle You mean 'e fancies me?

Speck Affirmative.

The crew relax

Suey Tlansporter loom leady, sir.
Paddy I'll monitor instruments, sir.

He exits through the slide door

Alura What is your plan, Captain?
Sam Simplicity itself.
Alura Simplicity?
Sam Invisibility.
Alura Invisibility?
Sam You guessed.
Pearl The molecular invisibility capsules, Captain? (*She produces a tin from her kind-aid box*)
Sam Exactly. We shall beam down to a predetermined spot but the molecular formation will not be reconstructed.
Mohammed Holy tablets!
        They'll be lookin' for somethin'
        And won't see nuffin'.
Suey (*pointing to the audience*) Shall we take all personnel in toulist section, Captain?
Lolita Yeah. We might need reinforcements.
Sam Of course.
Dazzle Ooooo. You're comin' wiv us.
Sam Bones.
Mohammed (*gyrating across*) "Dem bones dem bones dem dry bones."
Sam Instruct them.

The crew mime actions to the verse

Mohammed (*to the audience*)
        When I start yappin'
        Keep ya big ears flappin'
        Inside your programme
        You'll have seen
        A great big tablet
        Coloured green.
Alura Please take the green tablet from the Space Pak Programme. (*See Production Notes*)
Pearl It is imperative that you take this tablet.
Lolita At the precise moment you hear the code word.
Mohammed Uncle Jim.
Speck Uncle Jim?
Mohammed Yeah. It's a family show.
Speck Good thinking.
Lolita I'll guard the ship. (*She totes a gun*) Anything they can do I can do better.

Crew (*singing*) She can do anything better than them. (*Suddenly back to normal*)
Pearl Take care now.
Alura I'd come myself but my hair is such a mess.
Sam To the transporter room.

Sam, Speck, Mohammed and Dazzle cross to the transporter tubes

Ready, Mr Suey.
Suey Switch going upee.
Sam Ready to beam downee.

They take communications from hooks inside the tubes

Mohammed Keep those tablets very handy.
                 In the middle of your pandy.
Sam Five ... four ... three ... two ... one ...
Mohammed Uncle Jim.

They all swallow their tablets

Energize.

The Lights oscillate and Sam, Speck, Mohammed and Dazzle all shiver their bodies. Black-out. We see them again when the lights come up on the area B. They are in a frozen group à la Star Trek. They jolt into action; slow motion

Scan area

They flick open communicators and then use them as powder compacts while they powder faces and titivate hair in mirrors. Then scan the area

Speck Temperature level red alert, sir.
Sam Reading of eight thousand degrees centigrade.
Mohammed Holy hot dogs.

They all show heat discomfort

Dazzle (*looking in compact mirror*) Blimey, me mascara's gone all runny.
Sam Coolers on.

They press invisible buttons on their costumes

The audience become aware of sexy robot females holding guns entering as the Lights go red. They are Bolshies. They move like robots, speak like Daleks

Speck Instruments recording energy but not life form.
Dazzle (*spotting Bolshies*) Blimey. Look at them.
Mohammed Are dey Daleks?
Sam No. Daleks became extinct after the rabies outbreak of 1980.
Dazzle They look nasty.
Sam Yes. If my recognition training has not failed me these look suspiciously like ... (*he can't remember*) like ... er ...
Speck Bolshies?

Sam Correct.
Speck Controlled by neuro-magnetic valves.
Mohammed Don't worry they can't see us.
Little Volga (*like a Dalek*) Do—not—move.
Bolshie 1 We—have—our—sting—rays—
Bolshie 2 —trained—on—you—
Sam Do—as—they—say. (*He unwittingly copies their delivery*)

The Bolshies surround them and take them prisoner. When they move they make little sounds that sound suspiciously like the word "bolshy"

Big Olga enters flanked by two guards at the slide doors

Big Olga So, Captain you haf met the roboserfs.
Sam They made us very welcome.
Mohammed Say, how come all your crew is female?
Big Olga Vee are a women's liberation ship.
Dazzle Ay ay.
Little Volga Quiet capitalist traitor.
Speck Logically I assume that you require something of us?
Big Olga Ah. Ze famous Mister Specknik. Direct as ever.
Bolshies Let—us—destroy—them. Let—us—destroy—them.
Little Volga Enough.

They make small whispering sounds

Ozzervise no rugby this evenink.

They squeak in disappointment

Big Olga Destruction later. First ve require your skills.
Sam Skills?
Big Olga Let me be briefski. Our main power plant is malfunctionink. Zere iz only vone engineerski in space brilliant enough to correct it.
Dazzle Not Mr Paddy?
Big Olga Exactly.
Sam But the man is a half-wit.
Big Olga It's only a part-time job.
Little Volga And ve must have power.
Bolshies (*crescendo*) Power. *Power.*
Sam You wish to change the face of space?
Big Olga Da. Come ze glorious evolution.

Big Olga sings while Little Volga and the Bolshies do a space Russian dance and sing. Later the crew unwittingly get caught up in the wild Cossack fervour and join in

Song 5: Come Ze Glorious Evolution

(*singing*)   Come
                     Zee glorious evolution
                     Und

Zee Bolshy revolution
Mit ze power vee create
Vee shall change zee shape of space
Come zee
Glorious evolution

Big Olga
Bolshies   We shall all march togezzer
Hand in hand und side by side. Hi!
Ve shall go togezzer
Inside out und vith zee tide. Hi!
Vee shall stand togezzer
Back to back und upside down
Vee shall all run togezzer
In and out und round und round. Hi!

Big Olga   In
Zee twinkling off an eye
Vee'll haf
A Red Star paradise
Everyone vill haf a yacht
Vhezzer zey want a yacht or not
Come zee
Glorious evolution

Big Olga
Bolshies   We shall all march togezzer
Hand in hand und side by side. Hi!
Ve shall go togezzer
Inside out und vith zee tide. Hi!
Vee shall stand togezzer
Back to back und upside down
Vee shall all run togezzer
In and out und round und round. Hi!

Big Olga   On
Zee planets near and far
There'll be
A Red Star *coup d'état*
A few vodka bombs in space
Will wipe the Smirnoff
Off your face

Big Olga
Bolshies   Come
Zee glorious evolution
Vee shall all march togezzer
Hand in hand und side by side. Hi!
Vee shall go togezzer
Inside out und vith zee tide. Hi!
Vee shall stand togezzer
Back to back und upzide down
Vee shall all run togezzer
In und out und round und round.
Vee shall all run togezzer
In und out und round und round

Yes ve'll all run togezzer
In und out
Und
Round und round! Hi!

Reprise in double time

Big Olga Unt now beam down your engineerski.
Sam Space fiend. You mean to rewrite the History of Time.
Big Olga On Red Star all ze history books have loose leafs.
Speck Economical as well as logical, sir.
Dazzle (*to the audience*) Saves a lotta trouble don' it?
Mohammed (*to Sam*) Stay loose, man.
Sam (*turning on them with a ham flourish*) Fools. Don't you realize it will never stop there. Today—Red Star. Tomorrow—the Encyclopaedia Galactica.

The others gasp

Dazzle (*screaming*) No!
Little Volga Yes!

She and the Bolshies cackle

Big Olga makes a signal and the noise ceases

Big Olga Enough. Ze engineer. Or the girl dies.
Sam You leave me little choice. (*He flicks open his communicator*) Galactic to starship. Mr Suey?
Suey (*from the starship*) Healing you velly clear, Claptain.
Sam Mr Suey, beam down Paddy immediately.
Suey Energizing now, sir.

The Lights dip and when they come up we see the frozen figure of Paddy with razor in hand, cream on face and holding a towel. He is wearing space pants and vest

Paddy (*jolting to life*) I'm sorry, Captain but you caught me somewhat underwears. I was in the middle of me shaving.
Little Volga Ha. Still using primitive methods I see.
Paddy (*to Little Volga*) No sir. It's stubble stripper supplied by Duotronic Household Goods.

Jingle G: No need for comb no need for clipper, with Duotronic Stubble Stripper

The Bolshies all laugh like the robots in the instant mashed potato ad

Big Olga Silencikoff.
Sam Paddy. Your engineering skills are required.
Paddy But I'm an unknown failure, sir.
Sam Now's your chance to become a famous failure.
Dazzle Fink you can do it, Paddy?

Paddy Well I——
Big Olga (*grabbing him by the scruff of the neck*) Our neuro-magnetic power centre requires immediate treatment.
Bolshies Treatment.
Big Olga Repair it.
Bolshies Repair it.
Little Volga Or the girl gets Kremlined.
Bolshies Kremlined.
Mohammed Dey ain't foolin', man.
Paddy (*to Sam*) May I have a few words privately, sir?
Sam (*to Big Olga*) B.O.?
Big Olga Very well. Twenty space ticks only.
Little Volga The girl stays. (*To Bolshies*) Stingrays on kill.
Bolshies On kill. (*They train their guns on Dazzle*)
Dazzle Don't worry about me, Sam. I gotta do me nails anyway.

She starts to paint her nails which fascinates the Bolshies. Paddy, Speck, Sam and Mohammed go into a conspiratorial huddle side stage

Speck (*whispering*) Paddy. You have a plan?
Paddy I do, sir. Have you got some pepper?
Sam Black pepper or white pepper?
Paddy No sir. Writing pepper.
Mohammed Here. (*He produces a piece of paper*)
Paddy Good. Now I estimate that there are exactly one tousand and tirty-tree operable Bolshies on Red Star. (*Using the pencil behind Speck's ear*)
Speck Incredible. How did you deduce this figure?
Paddy Simple sir. I just counted their legs and then divided by two.
Speck This fool is a genius.
Sam The plan?
Paddy Well sir, I believe these creatures feed on small pieces of metal.
Sam (*confirmation*) Bones?
Mohammed That is their staple diet, sir.
Speck I think I can guess your strategy.
Sam Reverse the polarity force fields?
Paddy You've got it.
Speck Beam a phaser on to their computer synapses?
Paddy Exactly.
Mohammed And they'll revert to human magnets.
Paddy Right.
Big Olga (*interrupting*) Your time is upski. Finish zee job.
Paddy Certainly sir. (*He flicks open his communicator*) Mr Suey, a directional reading on Red Star magneto base.
Suey Reading eight-nine-five point fifty-five.
Paddy Tank you Mr Suey. And now ...
Big Olga Vot are you doinsk?
Paddy Fire phaser one.
Suey Firing as lequested.
Big Olga No.

We hear a phaser being fired, there are explosions as the magneto explodes. The Lights go up and down. There are screams etc. and we see the Bolshies slowly being dragged closer and closer until they are all stuck together by hand, elbow, head or bum

Bolshies Out of control. Out of control.
Big Olga My synapses.
Dazzle Serve yer right.

Silence. They freeze

Sam Never meddle with democracy.

The noise and action continue

Bolshies Out of control. Out of control.
Little Volga Ve shall be like zis foreffer.
Big Olga Magnetic eternities.

They all scream and spin off. There is silence

Sam Beam us up, Mr Suey and make it fast!
Suey Bleaming up, Claptain.

The Lights fade. Then the Lights come up as we see Sam, Dazzle, Mohammed, Paddy and Speck standing in the transporter room tubes. They all quiver and giggle as they materialize

Alura You all right, Mr Speck?
Speck I am intact.
Pearl Mohammed?
Mohammed Unmolested.
Lolita Paddy?
Paddy A close shave.

He points to his chin and Pearl sticks a plaster over a supposed cut

Dazzle 'Ome sweet 'ome, Sam.

They all move into the starship interior

Sam Indeed. Well done, Paddy.
Paddy (*as he exits*) Sure twas nothin' sir. The more you understand the less you realize you know.

Paddy exits

Speck Loony, but logically challenging.
Alura Standing by to move out of orbit, sir.
Sam Warp factor six.
Mohammed Now we're in the sky and riding high, I'll be away to my sick bay.

As he moves to the slide doors, Pearl sticks a thermometer in his mouth

Mohammed exits

Sam We shall rest. Revert to auto-control.
Lolita Auto-control on.
Sam Mr Suey. Mr Speck. Accompany me to the . . . analysis compound.
Suey Velly good.
Speck A small glass of sugar fermentation would be most acceptable, sir.

They exit "lads off to the local"

The ship seems suddenly quiet

Lolita (*quietly*) Ship on course for Procyon—safety catch up. (*She adjusts her gun*)
Alura Deflector shields off—eyelashes on. (*She sees to her eyes with mascara brush*)
Pearl Working lights down—energy pill in. (*She pops one in her mouth*)
Dazzle Shoes off! My feet are killin' me. (*After a pause*) 'Ere it's nice'n' quiet innit?
Pearl It's what we call time-slip time.

The Lights go down slowly; focus on the girls

Lolita You'll hear sounds in space you never heard before.
Dazzle Really?
Alura Sure thing. Look—a shooting star.
Dazzle Blimey that's really lovely.

Song 6: Space Angel

Dazzle, Lolita **Alura, Pearl**	Out there There's a sea of light and sound Up there There are angels flying round But like the spices in your hair They will melt into the air And the quiet will take your breath away Yes like the spices in your hair They will melt into the air And the quiet Will take your breath away But If you're A space dreamer, a peace seeker You will find If you're A space rocker, a time mocker You will touch Yes, you will touch and you will find The marble floors of paradise And the quiet Will take your breath away.

Out there
In the blue grey face of space.
Up there
Shine white pleasure domes of lace
But like bright candles in the sky
They will flicker and then die
And the quiet will take your breath away
Yes like bright candles in the sky
They will flicker and then die
And the quiet
Will take your breath away

But
If you're
A space dreamer, a peace seeker
You will find
If you're
A space rocker, a time mocker
You will touch
Yes, you will touch and you will find
The marble floors of paradise
And the quiet will
Take your
Breath
Away

There is a moment and the Lights come up slowly

Then the slide doors open and Mohammed's head comes round the door followed by Speck's and Suey's heads

Mohammed (*quietly*) Sure is quiet around here.
Speck Pastoral.
Suey Velly pleaceful.

Sam enters

Sam (*breaking the reverie*) Pleaceful or not, the pangs of hunger are gnawing at my vitals.
Dazzle (*back to normal*) I could do wiv some nosh meself.
Alura Tricorder on.
Pearl Stand by for readout.
Speck (*looking into the tricorder*) Co-ordinates on readout would suggest, Captain, that there is an Eastern take-away asteroid in close proximity.
All Yahoo!
Sam Mr Suey?
Suey Inflammation collect, Claptain.
Lolita What is it?
Suey Asteloid eight-nine-seven. Velly good Chinese take-away.
Mohammed Hmmm hmmmm, I can smell it already.
Pearl Hope it's nutritious.

Suey It belong to one of my honolable ancestors.

Sam Mr Suey. Beam up nine portions of twenty-six, twenty-seven and twenty-eight.

Dazzle Coo. Can I 'ave a pancake roll, Sam? I luve 'em.

Others (*ad lib*) Mmm—yes please—the greatest ... *etc.*

Sam (*stoically—looks like he's paying*) And nine pancake rolls.

Suey Velly good sir. Come in asteloid eight-nine-seven.

Indian Voice (*off*) Hallo. This is Asteroid eight-nine-eight. Ranjit's silicon chip and curry emporium.

Suey This not Asteloid eight-nine-seven?

Indian Voice (*off*) Oh my goodness no. This is Asteroid eight-nine-eight.

Suey Then please nip nex' door and order nine portions twenty-six, twenty-seven, twenty-eight and nine pancake rollee.

Indian Voice (*off*) Please not to get imperial knickers in twist. I am running there as fast as my legs are coming. Over, out and upwards.

Suey Flood (*food*) and waiter service on way, sir.

Alura Sweet 'n' sour space balls.

Pearl Spare ribs.

Lolita Karate chops.

Mohammed Mr Suey. I have been wondering. How come you people get such funny names? How come you don't have jist ordinary names like Mohammed McToxic?

Suey Velly intelesting question. Many years ago great Chinese philosopher Confusion, he say names derive from old Chinese clustom of parents throwing family cutlery into air and writing down name as they fall ... ping, chang, kung, suey.

Speck Illogical, Captain, but it seemed to amuse a small section of the audience.

Suey Here comes flood sir. Beaming up first-class Chinese foodee from old Uncle Sam Pan's space take-away.

Mohammed Sam Pan's sweet 'n' sour special.

During the song and dance tables are wheeled on, cloths laid, bottles with candles, candles are lit, chairs placed at each of the tables, plates brought in and placed. Non-serving waiters have fans

Song 7: Velly Velly Tastee Too

Tables are wheeled in

Suey   Sam Pan
                     Special fried rice
                     Special fried rice
                     Special fried rice, egg foo.
                     We sell at vellee cheap price
                     Specially fried for you.

Tablecloths are placed

Chinese Waiters All our food

Vellee vellee good
Vellee vellee tasty too!
Chicken chow mein
Puts hairs on chest
Vellee good for dandruff too!
Vellee vellee tasty
Vellee vellee tasty
Velle vellee tasty
Fried rice

Candles are placed on the tables

Suey   After tea
Try lychee
Fresh from Shanghai shopee
No ole lubbish like you get
At Tesco or Co-opee

The candles are lit

Chinese Waiters   All our food
Vellee vellee good
Vellee vellee tasty too!
Egg fried rice
In Chinese wall
Vellee good as concrete too
Vellee vellee tasty
Vellee vellee tasty
Vellee vellee tasty
Fried rice

Plates are placed

Suey   Crispy noodle
Chinese pork
Bamboo shoot in batter
Not mushroom
For curry sauce
Or chu chin chow
Prawn cracker

Chairs are placed

Chinese Waiters   All our food
Vellee vellee good
Vellee vellee tasty too!
Egg fried rice
In Chinese wall
Vellee good as concrete too
Vellee vellee tasty
Vellee vellee tasty
Vellee vellee tasty

Fried rice

The crew sit at the tables and start eating

Suey   Yesterday
                            Vellee big man
                            Call out "Waitee, Waitee"
                            He say "This soup plate vellee vellee damp"
                            I say, "That *is* the soupee"
Chinese Waiters   All our food
                            Vellee vellee good
                            Vellee vellee tasty too
                            Yangtze yum-yums
                            Vellee yellee tough
                            But velly good for sole of shoe
                            Velly good for sole of
                            Velly good for sole of
                            Vellee good for sole of shoe
                            Kung fu

*At the end of the song all the Waiters disappear including, surreptitiously,
Dazzle*

The crew are tucking into food with silver space sticks

Mohammed This is really sumthin'
Alura Deeee-licee.
Lolita Scrumee.
Pearl Noshee.

There is a scream off-stage and a horrible laugh

  Paddy rushes through the slide doors

Paddy Sir. Sometink dreadful!

They all leap up

Sam Dreadful?
Paddy Miss Dazzle has been snatched.

All scream

Sam Snatched?
Paddy Kidnapped, sir, by an Irish astral pirate.

They run across to Paddy

Mohammed How d'ye know he was Irish?
Paddy He had a patch over both eyes.
Sam (*to the audience*) The fiend!

They all freeze and scream, holding their poses in agonized shape as . . .

  Gary Gemini and Angela Krypton zip in through the slide door

During the speech the Lights fade on the crew and they exit in the darkness

Gary Yes, HomeWorld people. Why has Dazzle Star been snitched, er—snatched?

Angela Is Big Olga really Sam Galactic's stepmother?

Gary Who is Slimebag the Haemorrhage?

Angela Take the blue tranquillizer in your space pak now . . .

They pop one in the mouth

Gary . . . and relax.

They go into a sudden clinch. They kiss. Angela breaks from it and says out front

Angela Gary . . . I'll give you just fifteen minutes to stop doing that.

They immediately go into a clinch again as the Lights fade. The house lights come up

Jingle H: See you soon for part two

TOUCH DOWN

Jingle I: Welcome back to Homeworld X95

The Lights come up to reveal Gary and Angela in a clinch

Angela (*out of breath*) Time's up!

Gary (*smoothie*) Hope you had as much fun as we did.

Angela And now Duotronic video retro-scan will remind you of those nail-biting moments at the end of Blast Off.

Gary You're gonna see it all again in colour replay.

Angela Flick the Pic-Flicks.

> *As they speak, the crew enter and adopt the identical freeze positions they held at the end of the first half at "The Fiend!" We hear the jingle below and they all move backwards at speed to imaginary chairs as if the video film is being run backwards for a rerun. The sequence is then replayed in slow motion with the movements and the voices dragging. Meanwhile Angela and Gary exit*

Jingle J: We've got the pic-flicks in the can with Duotronic retroscan

Paddy Sir s-o-m-e-t-i-n-k d-r-e-a-d-f-u-l.

Sam D-r-e-a-d-f-u-l?

Paddy M-i-s-s D-a-z-z-l-e h-a-s b-e-e-n s-n-a-t-c-h-e-d.

Sam S-n-a-t-c-h-e-d?

Paddy K-i-d-n-a-p-p-e-d b-y a-n I-r-i-s-h a-s-t-r-a-l p-i-r-a-t-e.

Sam H-o-w -d-i-d y-o-u k-n-o-w h-e w-a-s I-r-i-s-h?

Paddy H-e h-a-d a p-a-t-c-h o-v-e-r b-o-t-h e-y-e-s.

All (*to the audience*) T-h-e f-i-e-n-d! (*They all scream*)

There is a sudden dipping of the Lights and the crew jolt back on to the ship interior at normal speed. They appear to be flung across the ship

Lolita Celestial Bazookas.

Pearl We're under attack.

The Lights go up and down, the alert sounds

Speck Photon torpedoes.

Sam Red alert.

Alura Something in my impulse vent, sir.

Sam We've got no time for personal matters.

Suey Two more torpedoes on target. (*He puts on a Second World War tin helmet*)

Speck Ear muffs on sir. (*He clips on two protective ear headphones*)

Paddy (*displaying a bottle*) Space-Scotch intact sir.
Pearl Hairnets on.

They all put on hairnets except Suey

Mohammed Hold on baby! Here dey come!

There are two torpedo explosions. The crew are jolted from one side of the ship to the other. There are a number of injuries

Sam Reinforcements Pearl, apply plasters and patch.

Pearl starts to put plasters on Paddy and especially Mohammed and then attacks some parts of the ship

Speck Locking phasers on target.
Suey Phasers ineffectual, sir.
Lolita We appear to be held in a force field, sir.
Paddy Begorrah, worse than that.
Lolita Worse?
Paddy Look. (*He holds up a piece of green plastic and wipes it on his tunic*)
Speck No.
Alura Not.
Sam Yes.
Paddy (*slowly*) A slime field.

Crash of menacing music

Speck Logically that can mean only one person.
Sam Slimebag the Haemorrhage.

> *There is a burst of electronic sound mingled with slimy bubbling and hideous laughter. The crew freeze as the main playing area is flooded with green light and the Slimeys swamp and slime on to the area. They carry water pistols. They actually make contact with the audience, sliming over them. They are led by Slimebag and his creepy sidekick Swampey. Slimebag has two black patches over his eyes. They are pantomimic but frightening. Slimebag has a hook in place of the right hand and Swampey a hook for the left hand. The song and dance is executed in an inarticulate, stompy manner*

Song 8: The Slimey Swampers' Stomp

Slimebag	Desolation
Swampey	Devastation
	~~Across the seven astral seas.~~
	We will sap the sky's foundations
	Cataclysmic slime disease
	Multiply our procreation
	Wreck the starships
	Loot their holds
	Submerge the system
	Take control
	And do the Slimey Swampers' Stomp

Chorus	Stomp stomp stomp swamper stomp
	Stomp stomp stomp swamper stomp
	Find it, bind it
	Swamp it, slime it
	Wipe it off the face of time.
Slimebag	Annihilation
Swampey	Decimation
	Condemning them to purgatory
	Dazzle Star is in our power
	Death shall be her destiny
	Soon Galactic's crew will cower
	Cry for mercy
	Cringe with fear
	Walk the space plank
	And disappear
	As we stomp
	The Slimy Swampers' Stomp
Chorus	Stomp stomp stomp swampers stomp
	Stomp stomp stomp swamper stomp
	Find it, bind it
	Swamp it, slime it
	Wipe it off the face of time
	Wipe it off the face of time.

Slimebag (*concluding the song with a great laugh*) Squelch the girl in.
Swampey Immudiately, great slime.

All the Slimeys slurp about making slimy noises

  Dazzle is dragged in bound by seaweed

Dazzle 'Elp 'elp!
Slimebag Stop drizzling, girl.
Swampey Slurp up.
Dazzle Watcha gonna do.
Slimebag Give you a jab with the slimodermic.

They all slurp and gurgle with laughter

Swampey Here it is. (*He produces a green hypo—large*)
Dazzle No. no.
Slimebag Yes yes.
Swampey (*jabbing it in*) There——

Dazzle passes out

  —that should keep her dampened down for a bit.
Slimebag Tie 'er to that seaweed.
Swampey What seaweed?

Either a coil of seaweed almost magically appears pulled by a line from the grid, or a Slimey may be used

Slimebag That seaweed.

All the Slimeys applaud slime-fashion

Swampey Ooze gonna guard her, O great deluge?
Slimebag Couple of them squirts. (*Signalling to Slimeys*)
Swampey Slime 'er up over there quickly.
Slimebag I shall go below and write up the water-log and then wet and sea what the tide washes up.
Swampey Galactic eh, O damp one?
Slimebag Moist likely, drip.
Swampey Then we can get our hands on that Dazzle Star.
Slimebag Hooks.
Swampey Then we can get our hooks on that Dazzle Star. Make it part of the Klingon empire.

They brandish their hooks

Slimebag And my reign will continue forever.
Swampey A torrential rain eh, O magnificent slobber?
Slimebag Shut yer drain cover stupid.
Swampey Listen.

Dead silence, long pause

Slimebag What?
Swampey Nothin'.
Slimebag (*to the audience*) Water on the brain. (*Signifying Swampey's stupidity*)
Swampey There it is again.
Slimebag You're right. It's Galactic's underwater shuttlecock coming down to the astral mud. Quick. Under cover and out of slime. The trap is baited.

Laughter and slimy noises and they form rock shapes etc.

Slimebag and Swampey exit

Song 9: Honolulu Lulu

Crew (*swimming or dancing across the stage*)	Swimming to you Across the surging coral Flying to you Through the hazy blue Be my Honolulu Lulu And when I reach that shore That green pacific shore
Slimeys (*suddenly rising with Hawaiian garlands or leis and swaying*)	I'll hold you in my arms again Ooo waki waki waki ooo ooo ooo Ooo waki waki waki ooo ooo ooo Ooo waki waki wakity waki waki Ooo waki waki waki ooo ooo ooo
Crew	Striving for you From Venus to Hawaii Sighing for you

By the blue lagoon
Be my underwater lover
'Cos if you'll be my beau
I'll be your Jacques Cousteau
And hold you in my arms again

Slimeys Ooo waki waki waki ooo ooo ooo
Ooo waki waki waki ooo ooo ooo
Ooo waki waki wakity waki waki
Ooo waki waki waki ooo ooo ooo.

Crew Diving for you
In the deepest ocean
Sailing to you
Across the deep blue sea
Be my own bikini sweetie
And like Helen's lips
I'll launch a thousand ships
To hold you in my arms again
Ooo ooo
I'll hold you in my arms again

Slimeys Ooo waki woo

During the last verse and chorus Dazzle is released by Sam

Sam Dazzle, you are safe.
Dazzle (*to the audience*) I bet he tries to kiss me now.
Sam (*taking her in his arms*) Dazzle.
Dazzle (*putting her hand over his lips*) You mustn't. People are looking.
Sam (*gritty*) I must.
Dazzle (*to the audience*) Well at least I resisted. (*She winks but their kiss is forestalled as . . .*)

Slimebag and Swampey enter

Slimebag Surround 'em.
Swampey Maroon 'em.
Slimebag (*spotting Sam's arms around Dazzle*) And enough of this wet stuff.
Swampey Wading.
Slimebag Wallowing in love muck.

Slimeys make "ugh" sound

Swampey Hand over the dazzle defender.
Sam You will never take her.
Slimebag Not the girl you dozy dribble.
Swampey The star. The dazzle star.
Sam I don't understand.
Mohammed Me neither.
Speck It would appear that our HomeWorld guest has given us insufficient data.
Dazzle Right Specky. This is what they want. (*She picks up the star, secreted behind the raised area upstage*)

Slimeys draw back slightly afraid. A follow spot focuses on the star

Slimebag Don't go green at the gills.
Swampey She can't activate it without the——
Speck Computer sphere?
Slimebag Right. So just hose it over here or you'll find a watery grave at the end of a squirt gun jet.
Swampey Cover 'em.

The girls scream, the Slimeys fire water pistols into the audience

Slimebag Hand over the dazzle star.
Dazzle Never.
Sam I think ... that I am totally confused by this conversation.
Dazzle You will never control its power, slimy sluicepump.
Slimebag What did she call me?
Swampey She called you a slimy sluice—
Slimebag Shut up stupid.
Dazzle Look. I shall hurl it into space. Beyond time where you will never find it.

She passes the star secretly to Alura who hides it behind Suey's panel. The audience do not see this. Dazzle then pretends to throw the star and the Lights dim as we hear the sound of the star hurtling through time. A follow spot follows its supposed track

Slimebag No. *No.*
Crew Yes. *Yes.*
Sam It would appear that your space piracy is at an end, Haemorrhage.
Slimebag (*stepping forward*) Ha! And what do you think you can do, Galactic?
Sam (*stepping towards him*) Ha! What do I think I can do ... (*he pauses, his smile vanishes, he hasn't a clue*) ... what do I think I can do, Speck?
Speck Assuming this is a normal astral sea floating in a slime force field.
Alura We would merely have to pull out the hydrotic stopper sir.
Sam Hydrotic stopper?
Speck This is part of a black hole.
Lolita Just pull out the plug, sir.
Pearl The inward gravitational effect will drag them into the eye of the sky.
Sam Giving us time to finish the show?
Speck Something like that, sir.
Slimebag Watcha whispering about, dribbles?
Dazzle Your end, sluice bog.
Slimebag What!
Swampey She called you a sl—
Slimebag Shut up.
Sam Paddy, the plug.
Paddy Right, sir.

The crew gather and in mime grunt and groan as they pull an invisible plug out of the floor. We hear a loud pop as if a plug had been pulled out of a bath. This is followed by quadrophonic sound of water rushing down the waste. The Lights flash

Slimebag and the Slimeys all give horrible screams and whirl around as they disappear off the set

The crew whirl in the opposite direction and when the Lights steady we find them in position aboard the starship

Suey (*at the console*) Moving out of orbit.
Alura Black hole receding.
Speck (*looking out to the central area*) Fascinating. Unbelievable.
Sam Mr Speck?
Speck I distinctly saw a rubber duck, sir.
Sam Illogical.
Lolita Starship stable.
Pearl All frequencies transmitting.
Mohammed (*scanning the area*) Slime infection decreasing.
Dazzle That was a close one, Sam.
Sam Indeed and now an explanation is required.
Dazzle Well . . .
Alura HomeWorld transmission coming through, sir.
Pearl It's the president, Captain.
Suey Audio on.

Sekurikor comes up on the video screen

Sekurikor Galactic.
Sam Sekurikor.
Sekurikor An apology for not informing you of the real purpose of your mission. Security demanded the utmost secrecy.
Dazzle Sorry Sam.
Speck No finishing school on Procyon?
Sekurikor A mere ruse. Procyon has no more than a few tobacco fields planted there in the twenty-first century by——
Speck Two of our early exploratory space commanders.
Dazzle Benson and Hedges?
Sekurikor Just so. But Procyon *could* be an ideal star for a *new* empire.
Sam (*standing lookout as at a new opportunity*) A new millenium?
Sekurikor Exactly. HomeWorld is running out of resources. Becoming fast exhausted.
Paddy We need to create a new place for our civilization.
Sekurikor Certainly, but it must be a *safe* place.
Dazzle Completely protected from aliens like Haemorrhage.
Sekurikor That is why my daughter was transporting the fabulous dazzle star to Procyon.
Mohammed The dazzle star?
Sekurikor Yes. Once placed in the computer sphere on Procyon it radiates a defence force field of incredible power.
Sam Impenetrable?

Sekurikor Completely.
Alura What does this word D-A-Z-Z-L-E stand for?
Sekurikor Defender of All Zenith Zones——
Crew (*repeating*) Defender of All Zenith Zones . . .
Sekurikor —and—a Little Extra.
Crew Wow!
Dazzle Colonial freighters are already transporting HomeWorld people to Procyon.
Mohammed But they won't have no protection.
Sekurikor That is right. So you see it is imperative that the star be retrieved or they are open to alien attack.
Lolita Doomed.
Alura Get that star, Sam.
Suey This is a job for a space bore.
Pearl Use the time shoot.
Paddy While there's still time.
Lolita And save all humanity.

Sekurikor's image fades

Sam All personnel to standby. The bridge will be vacated and the time shoot prepared. This is a priority one order.

Most of the crew exit

Pearl. I shall require standard hero equipment.
Pearl Certainly, sir. (*She puts one of his arms in a sling and a bloodied headband round his forehead*)

Pearl exits

Dazzle (*out front*) In'e bloody?

Sam and Dazzle are alone

Sam Take out your recorder pad.

She takes out a notebook

This is important.
Dazzle Recorder pad ready.
Sam Can you do shorthand?
Dazzle Yeah . . . but it takes longer.
Sam Record this for posterity. (*He dashes heroically across to the microphone* R) Captain's log. Star date three-two-seven-two point six.

Song 10: Man Above All Men

(*singing*)   I am ready
                     To leap into time
                     Prepared to do and to die
                     Knowing that with you by my side
                     I can win. I can win.

> Yeah, I can win and come through
> Blaze a trail with you
> Light night's lanterns with you
> And be a man
> Above all men

Dazzle (*spoken*) Oh Sam. (*She throws aside her pad and sings*)

> I am longing
> To fly by your side
> Prepared to kiss life goodbye
> Knowing that with you by my side
> I am safe. I am safe
> Yeah, I am safe and secure
> Undaunted and sure
> Knowing you'll keep me pure
> And be my man
> Above all men.

Sam
> To all Starship commanders
> There comes the challenging call
> To every Starship mariner
> The chance to fight or fall
> To stand against disruptive force
> To combat infamy
> To stand and take whatever comes to you
> And face one's destiny

Sam So
Dazzle
> We are ready
> To leap into time
> Prepared to do and to die
> Knowing that with you by my side
> I can win.
> I can win.

Sam Yeah, I can win and come through
Dazzle Blaze a trail with you
Sam Light night's lanterns with you
Dazzle And be a man
> Above all men
> And be a man
> Above
> All
> Men

*They are together and about to kiss, but just as the lips are about to touch, they
turn heads to face the audience. The emotion is too much*

Voice (*off*) Prepare for time shoot.
Dazzle It's a big decision, Sam.
Sam Everything in my life is big.
Dazzle (*to the audience*) Pretty good in'e?

Sam We are both involved and committed to the task.
Dazzle Like eggs and bacon.

There is a moment. Has Sam heard it right?

Sam Eggs and bacon?
Dazzle Yeah. I mean wiv eggs a chicken's involved innit, but wiv bacon the pig's committed.

The Lights suddenly flash

Help!

They both whirl into time

Voice (*off; on echo*) Time shoot activated . . . time shoot activated . . . time shoot activated . . .

Gary Gemini enters through the slide door. He has a bloodied headband but is also on crutches. He goes over the top emotionally

Gary And so our two heroes tumble back in time. Hurtling down the catacombs of space. Searching for the dazzle star upon which the hopes of our entire HomeWorld people depend. (*He points to the audience*) You people. As the centuritrons tick by, Sam and Dazzle find that their star sensors—supplied by Dutronic Household Goods——

Jingle B: Duotronic

—are pulling them towards the old, earth year of nineteen hundred and sixty. (*He tears off his headband*) Could the star be somewhere here? (*He drops a crutch*) Will they be able to fit it into the computer sphere in time? (*He drops the other crutch*) Will it be the right size? (*He faints*)

Black-out, during which Gary exits

When the Lights come up again on the playing area Gary has gone and we see a Greasers' tableau. They are dressed in authentic gear with bikes, Cokes, chains and all the paraphernalia of Hell's Angels. They all have black freckles on their faces

Sam and Dazzle stumble into the area

This brings the Greasers to alerted life. They adopt aggressive positions

Dave Aggro.
Vic Bovver.
Dave You ain't from around here.
Brenda Strangers.
Rita Unlisted persons.
Dave Berks.
Vic You'd better go annuver way.
Brenda Home.
Rita To Mummy!

They all laugh sneeringly

Dave (*going to Sam*) Are you students?
Sam No, I am Captain Galactic of the starship Sunburster One.
Vic Ah. (*Knowledgeably*) Salvation Army eh?
Dazzle We're looking for a star.
Brenda Small?
Rita About this big? (*She shows the exact shape of the dazzle star*)
Vic Looks a bit like a star.
Dazzle That's it.
Dave That star belongs to our leader.
Vic Yeah. Sue Zuki.
Brenda Don't tangle wiv 'er, 'andsome.
Rita She's a bit temperamental.
Dazzle How d'ye mean?
Brenda Fifty per cent temper.
Rita Fifty per cent mental.
Vic We call 'er Wonder Woman.
Sam Your reason?
Vic We sometimes wonder if she's a woman.

There is suddenly a row off-stage as Sue Zuki enters. She can either enter on foot or motorbike depending on your stage size, ambition or whether the actress can ride a motor bike. For a laugh she could enter on a kid's tricycle tarted up to look like the real thing

Sue Zuki I. Ain't. 'Appy.
Vic Sorry, chief.
Sue Zuki Shut up, Vandal. (*She belts him*)
Vic I was only chattin' up the bird, chief.
Sue Zuki (*mimicking*) "I was only chattin' up the bird, chief." Why?
Vic Well it's just my natural sex appeal, innit?
Sue Zuki Sex appeal? *Sex appeal?* Do you know sunnink, Vandal? You've got about as much sex appeal as a road accident.

They all laugh

Vic Yeah but—(*He is silenced*)
Sue Zuki Shut up. (*She belts him. Turning to Sam and Dazzle*) Now. Wotcher lookin' for around 'ere, sunshine?

Sam flashes a mouth full of smiling teeth

Dazzle We're lookin' for——
Sue Zuki Not you, bubble gum. I'm talking to Steradent over there.

Sam closes his mouth suddenly

Sam Fair one.

Sue quite likes that but the Greasers laugh

Sue Zuki Shut it.
Sam We are searching for the dazzle star in the libraries of time.

The Greasers cringe on the word "library"

Sue Zuki Searchin'?
Dave Libraries?
Vic You mean?
Sue Zuki You read?
Sam Yes but——

They all shrink back in horror

Sue Zuki Books?
Dazzle Yes.
Sue Zuki Jist as I fought. Rita?
Rita Yeah.
Sue Zuki Whatja fink?
Rita Poofs.
Sue Zuki Right.

Song 11: Greasers' Gavotte

(*singing*)	You'd better get this straight kid
	You'd better get it right
	We ain't got time for long-haired gits
	Who don' know 'ow to fight!
	We greasers live for action
	Astride our silver bikes
	We're kick-start born
	To dice wiv death
	On the motorway
	Of life
Greasers	You've gotta 'ave a lotta aggro
	You've gotta 'ave a lotta poke
	You've gotta 'ave a lot
	Of you know what
	When yer duffin' up annuver bloke
Sue Zuki	You've gotta be nifty
	On yer Norton seven-fifty
	When the goin' gets really tough
	Don' be a fairy
	Like Mary down the dairy
	You gotta be a real tough nut.
	Yeah.
Greasers	You gotta 'ave a lotta aggro
	You've gotta 'ave a lotta poke
	You've gotta 'ave a lot
	Of you know what
	When yer duffin' up annuver bloke

Gavotte dance. They take off scarves and use them flamboyantly as hankies in the gavotte. The gavotte steps and forms should be adopted. This should be sung posh

Sue Zuki	When you're dressed up in yer levver gear
Principal Greasers	Any bloke who's nuffin' shakes wiv fear
and Greaserettes	And he gets a gashin'
	Really nasty thrashin'
	Knuckle-sandwich bashin' round the ear
	If an Aussie tries to drink your beer
	Never never smile or shed a tear
	Just you put the boot in
	Really nasty hoof in
	Rearrange his southern hemisphere
Greasers	'Cos you've gotta 'ave a lotta aggro
	You've gotta 'ave a lotta poke
	You've gotta 'ave a lot
	Of you know what
	When you're duffin' up annuver bloke
	You've gotta get away
	On your flashy B.S.A
	And think about your strengf and 'elf

Don't be a pansy
Like Ted and Andy Pandy
Try to pull the strings yerself

Yeah
You gotta 'ave a lotta aggro
You've gotta 'ave a lotta poke
You've gotta 'ave a lot
Of you know what
When you're duffin' up annuver bloke

Sue Zuki	If a traffic warden comes round 'ere
Principal Greasers	Sit astride your bike and give a sneer
and Greaserettes	Then tie 'er to a meter
	Newly painted meter
	Stick a parking ticket in 'er ear
	If a copper says "'Allo 'Allo
	Transport cafés everywhere will close"
	Simply bend 'is helmet
	Nail him to a pelmet
	Gently stuff 'is truncheon up 'is nose
Greasers	'Cos you've gotta 'ave a lotta aggro
	You've gotta 'ave a lotta poke
	You've gotta 'ave a lot
	Of you know what
	When you're duffin' up annuver bloke
	You've gotta get away
	On your flashy B.S.A
	And think about your strengf and 'elf
	Don't be a pansy
	Like Ted and Andy Pandy

> Try to pull the strings yerself
> Yeah
> You gotta 'ave a lotta aggro
> You've gotta 'ave a lotta poke
> You've gotta 'ave a lot
> Of you know what
> When you're duffin' up anuvver
> Thumpin' up another
> Duffin' up anuvver bloke
> Yeah

Dazzle Miss Sue, we don't want any trouble.

Sam We come in peace.

Sue Zuki Your mission?

Sam To reach where no hand has ever set foot before surrounded by a crack team of scientists in tight sweaters and thigh boots.

Greasers Cor.

Vic Can I come?

Dave Shut up, stoopid. (*He belts him*)

Sue Zuki (*producing the dazzle star from behind Suey's panel* L) Is this wot yer lookin' for?

Dazzle (*reaching for it*) Yes.

Sue Zuki Not so fast. We ain't givin' it away. We want sunnink in return.

Sam You may have anything you desire. What are your needs? Strength?

Sue Zuki Nah.

Rita Dave 'ere can tear the tops off Coke bottles wiv 'is nostrils.

Dave makes strange nostril noises

Sam Power?

Rita You must be jokin'.

Sam Exotic foods?

Vic I wouldn't mind a mixed grill. (*He gets belted*)

Rita Will you shut up, gormick.

Sam What then? Come lay your cards on the table.

Sue Zuki (*pulling out a card*) American Express?

Sam That'll be fine.

Sue Zuki OK. Tell him, Rita.

Pause

Rita (*quietly*) Pimples.

Sam Pimples?

Rita Pimples.

Sue Zuki Spots.

Dave Teenage torment.

Brenda Unsightly marks.

Vic (*reading from a card taken from his pocket*) We need a natural healing balm containing nourishing minerals that will ease away those tell-tale . . . (*he turns it over*) . . . blemishes.

Sam No sooner said than erased. (*He flips open his communicator*) Galactic to starship.

Suey (*off*) Receiving you loud and clear, Claptain.

Sam Mr Suey, beam down officer Speck and a full medical team.

Suey (*off*) Velly good, sir.

Vic (*amazed by it all*) He must be in the Magic Circle or sunnink.

The Lights dim down and when they come up we see Mohammed, Pearl, Speck and Paddy in white surgical gowns. They wear Red Cross hats except Paddy whose hat has a green cross. They jolt into life. Mohammed carries a large medical case marked "DUOTRONOPLAST—supplied by Duotronic Household Goods"

Speck We surmised that our presence was required, Captain.

Sam You surmised correctly, Speck. (*To Mohammed*) Bones?

Mohammed Ah-huh?

Sam A miracle cure is needed.

Mohammed Yes sir.

Pearl How exciting.

Sam (*turning to the Greasers*) Gentlemen, may I introduce Doctor Mohammed McToxic.

Dave Which doctor?

Pearl No he's fully qualified.

Dazzle Who's gonna be the guinea pig?

Sue Zuki Vandal. (*She belts him*)

Vic Oh no. Please. I 'ate the dentist's.

Sue Zuki All right I suppose I'd better do it.

The Greasers back off upstage

Paddy Don't worry, miss. You're in the safest hands.

Mohammed I got the knowledge and assurance.
               Hope you got your life insurance.

Speck Hold still.

Sam Anaesthetic, Speck.

Speck You mean the dreaded Vulcan Death Breath?

Sam Affirmative.

Speck As you say, Captain.

He exhales a sudden breath at Sue and she immediately collapses

Dazzle Ooo-er.

Greasers Blimey. (*ad lib*)

Speck Do not panic. My lungs were only on stun.

Sam (*to the Greasers*) Come. Let us discuss exchange terms in a quieter place.

Vic Right. Clear the way. This way, Elastic.

Sam Galactic!

Vic Well we've all got our problems, mate.

They exit

Mohammed, Pearl, Paddy and Speck are left with the inert body of Sue Zuki

Paddy We'd better start the examination.
Speck Use the neuro-scanner, Bones.
Mohammed Yes sir. (*He takes a battery-operated Kenwood Mixer from the bag and scans the body from the legs to the head*)
Pearl What is this strange growth on her neck?
Mohammed It's her head.
Pearl Oh.
Paddy What is your reading?
Mohammed The lady is suffering from tri-ox imbalance of body functions culminating in bio-compost eruption. In other words . . .
Speck Pimples.
Mohammed Exactly.
Paddy Here is the treatment. (*He pulls a bottle out of the case and points to it*)
Mohammed Duotronic Pimple Pulverizer.

They all point like an ad

Speck First let me check it. (*He tastes a little from the bottle on his finger*) Extraordinary. This liquid appears to have the consistency, smell and taste of whisky.
Paddy (*grabbing it and drinking*) Glory be, 'tis another miracle.
Mohammed It's for the patient.
Dazzle She's gawn all white.
Paddy Ghostly.
Dazzle I've never spoken to a spook, Speck; bring her round.

Speck clicks his fingers and Sue comes round

Sue Zuki 'Ere where am I, big ears?
Speck Safe with Noddy.
Pearl Quick, swallow this! (*She pours medicine down her throat*)
Paddy And now jump up and down.
Mohammed Jump up and down?
Paddy Sure. I forgot to shake the bottle.

The Lights dim as we see Sue Zuki and the rest jumping up and down. There is a momentary Black-out accompanied by chemical noises during which Sue quickly wipes the grease pimples off her face. Lights up. Her face is clear

Mohammed Baby, you're completely cured.
Pearl It works.
Speck (*flicking open his communicator as a mirror*) Look.
Sue Zuki Blimey that's fantastic. 'Ere 'ow did you do it?
Mohammed Co-efficiency.
Speck Symbiosis.
Paddy Helping one another.
Dazzle Being mates.

Song 12: Gotta Give a Guy a Helping Hand

Mohammed & Pearl	Ooohhh
Speck & Dazzle	Ooohhh
Paddy & Sue	Ooohhh
All	You'll find that life is pleasant
	If you work in harmony
Speck	Goodbye trouble
Paddy	Goodbye booze
All	Hallo sympathy
	Help your neighbour
	Give and take
	Work together
	Correlate
	Cut your slice
	But share your cake
	And live in harmonee-ee-ee
	Hand in hand
	That's the secret of life
	Hand in hand
	No friction or strife
	You'll find that things go right
	It's just like paradise
	If you always give a guy
	A helping hand
Mohammed & Pearl	Once we had a patient
	Who thought he was Moses
	Used to chase the nurses round with
	Out any clothes-es
	Which only goes to show that life's
	A bed of neuroses
All	So you've gotta give a guy
	A helping ha ha ha hand
	You've gotta give a guy
	A helping hand
Paddy	A friend of mine called Murphy
	Was an actor, OK.
Speck	The audience shouted "Pat
	Do somethin' Irish today"
Paddy	So he demolished the the-atre
	And dug up a motorway
All	'Cos you've gotta give a guy
	A helping ha ha ha hand
	Yeah, you've gotta give a guy
	A helping hand
Sue Zuki	So if the coppers caught me
	Nicking knick-knacks from shops
Dazzle	And nicked you with those knick-knacks

Right there on the job?

Sue Zuki (*speaking*) Yes.

Dazzle	We'd slip 'em arf a nicker
	And then knick-knacker off
All	'Cos you've gotta give a guy
	A helping ha ha ha hand
	Yeah, you've gotta give
	A digit-shovin'
	Extra special
	Ever lovin'
	Gotta give a guy
	A helping hand
	Yeah!

At the end of the song Sam enters with Dave, Vic, Rita and Brenda

Sam Gentlemen, you have dematerialized the problem?
Paddy The anti-matter has been destroyed, sir.
Dazzle The trade can be made.
Pearl Our star for your pimples.
Sue Zuki 'And it over, Reet.

Rita does so then sidles up to Mohammed

Rita You betcha. (*To Speck*) And I could really fancy 'im.
Speck I have scruples.
Sue Zuki I've been vaccinated.
Mohammed There's no time to lose sir.
Dazzle (*taking a card from Vic's pocket and reading*) No ... for we must return the star to the computer sphere on Procyon so that it may protect all earth creatures from the brittle world of death.
Vic (*snatching it back*) Yeah ... Well we're gonna be pretty busy this afternoon as well.
Rita Kicking old ladies.
Dave Duffin' up vicars.
Brenda Sprayin' cats.
Vic Nickin' fruit gums.
Sue Zuki (*belting him*) Leave orf, Vandal.
Sam We shall miss you but ... duty calls.
Dave Yeah—well look after yourself, OK?
Sue Zuki (*to Speck*) And you big ears.
Speck Emotive small-talk has no effect on me.
Sue Zuki Well if ever you decide to have a lobe-otomy let me know.
Speck Both irrational and unhygienic.
Sam Beam us up, Mr Suey.
Suey (*off*) Bleaming up, Claptain.
Dazzle 'Bye Sue.
Pearl And thanks.
Paddy A million.

Sue Zuki See yer around. (*Looking back at the Greasers*) Right?
Greasers Right.

They freeze as the Lights on the central area fade

> *The Lights come up on the interior of the ship. As the crew leave the transporter tubes Alura and Lolita come out of the slide door to meet them*

Dazzle Anybody home?
Alura Dazzle. Welcome back.
Lolita Did yer bust 'em wide open?
Sam On the contrary—
Speck (*interrupting*) I simply extended the hand of cosmic kindness.
Lolita You didn't need to annihilate them with unimaginable ferocity?
Speck No, I did it all on my own.
Alura By yourself?
Speck (*conceited*) Solus.
Sam Miss Pacemaker?
Pearl Sir?
Sam A vanity tranquillizer for Mr Speck.
Pearl Immediately sir. (*She places a large strip of plaster across his mouth*)
Sam And now proceed to maximum distance orbit, Suey.
Suey Velly good, sir.
Sam And remember, Speck. Anything you can do, I can do better.
Paddy He can do anything better than you.
Speck (*muffled*) No he can't.
Sam Yes I can! (*As if addressing a dog*) Heel!

They all freeze in begging positions

That's better. Now back to work.

They all start to busy themselves with instruments and Speck removes the plaster

Alura (*doing her face*) Nivea cream applied, Captain.
Lolita Armaments armed.
Pearl Surgical appliances applied.
Paddy Nuts and bolts loosened.
Sam Loose? Well tighten them.
Paddy That'll mean a screwdriver, sir.
Sam Well you're a mechanic, aren't you?
Paddy No, sir, I'm a McArthur, sir. The McAnnex are on me sister's side of the family.
Sam Just do it.
Paddy Yes sir. (*He starts to tighten dummy screws on the ship*)
Sam Mohammed.
Mohammed Sir?
Sam Answer the flight pattern bell.
Mohammed It's not ringing, sir.

Suddenly a bell rings

Sam Must you leave everything to the last moment?
Dazzle (*to the audience*) Fantastic, in'e.
Alura On course for the planet Procyon. (*She stands*)
Suey (*standing*) Holding steady.
Mohammed Course reading.
Others "A" OK. (*They all stand looking out front*)

Song 13: Comin' Back

Sam	Just around the bend
Dazzle	Is the journey's end
	And the sky is singin' my song
	'Cos it's just a stone's throw
	From the people I know
	Woh I'm comin' back to where I belong
	You gotta believe it
	I'm comin' back to where I belong.
Men	It may be true that those stars above us are worlds
	And a thousand times the earth in size
	But then all that I know when I'm comin' home
	Is what I see in the limit of my eyes.
All	Just around the bend
	Is the journey's end
	And the sky is singin' my song
	'Cos it's just a stone's throw
	From the people I know
	Woh I'm comin' back to where I belong
	You gotta believe it
	Yeah I'm comin' back to where I belong.
Girls	When we see the stars melt in the eager sun
	And the evening is red with clouds
	Like flags on a ship, they spell the end of a trip
	And we really want to shout out loud
All	Just around the bend
	Is the journey's end
	And the sky is singin' our song
	'Cos it's just a stone's throw
	From the people we know
	Woh we're comin' back to where we belong
	Yeah stop the world
	We wanna get off
	We're comin' back, comin' back, comin' back,
	To where we belong

The Lights start to change slightly

Speck Entering Procyon atmosphere.
Alura (*dabbing scent behind her ear*) Perfume applied.
Lolita Ten hemo-ticks to touchdown.

Pearl Check pulse arrest.

They all check wrist pulse. Sound effect of landing

Suey Starship reverberating.
Speck Preparing for re-entry shock.
Dazzle 'Old on.
Mohammed Gravitational plates buckling.
Pearl (*sticking cross patches on the ship*) Elastoplast repairing.
Sam Engine room?
Paddy Evostick holding firm, sir.
Alura Impact with rest pad . . . NOW.

The crew all jolt forward and then are still

Lolita We did it.
Mohammed No matter where you wander
　　　　　　　No matter where you roam
　　　　　　　Ain't no place better in dis world
　　　　　　　Than good ole home sweet home.

They all hug and congratulate each other ad lib

Speck Clear working platform.
Sam Miss Lolita, open the main stabilizing door.

Lolita steps forward and spits on her hands; then in mime, accompanied by huge grinding and squeaking noises, opens the door

Dazzle Blimey, 'ow can she move weights like that?
Pearl Polystyrene.
Dazzle Oh yeah. (*To the audience*) In' she terrific.

As the crew dismount from the ship and enter the central playing area . . .

　Sekurikor and Ministar enter through the slide door R

Sekurikor Welcome to Procyon, Sam Galactic.
Ministar Welcome to you and your magnificent crew.
Sam Thank you sir. It was . . . (*he grits his teeth*) . . . quite a trip.
Crew Yeah.
Ministar Your modesty belies the incredible difficulty of your achievement, Galactic.
Sam Well, it's difficult to be humble when you're as good as I am.
Sekurikor Oh. Allow me to introduce our keeper of the peace, Ministar the Astronomer.
Paddy How's work?
Ministar Looking up.
Paddy Good.

The computer sphere is rolled in

Sekurikor You have the dazzle star?

Dazzle (*changing to a perfect Roedean accent*) Here Daddy. All super safe and sound.

The crew step back stunned

Mohammed Am I crazy, am I sane
              But didn't Dazzle's voice just change?
Ministar So my dear, you've decided to drop your cover.
Sam Cover?
Sekurikor My daughter is one of our best peace agents, Galactic.
Dazzle I'm so sorry, Samuel, but I had to adopt the role of a simple lass so that you would not be emotionally attracted to me in any way, thus remaining morally and ethically——

They all go up on their toes as she says the next word

——intacta——

They go down again

——dedicated only to the acquisition of the dazzle star. Oh, Samuel, can you ever forgive me?
Sam (*gritting his teeth*) I . . . understand.
Dazzle (*to the audience*) Oh God. Isn't he spiffing?
Sekurikor And now to place the star in the computer sphere.

A follow spot follows the star

Ministar Thus completing a circle of peace and protection around our new earth.
Speck Allow me. (*He places the star on top of the sphere which starts to pulse and make a pulsing sound*)
Alura It fits.
Lolita Perfectly.
Sekurikor So your mission is completed.
Ministar Our tale nearly told.
Sekurikor Nevertheless we do have one more pleasant duty to perform.
Ministar The accolade?
Sekurikor Of course.

The crew kneel as the Lights dim and the spot follows Ministar to the steps in front of the sliding door

Ministar Sam. (*He unrolls the scroll which drops down and smashes on his foot. He screams*) Sam, from this day forth you are to hold the rank of admiral.
Crew (*sotto voce, wonder*) Admiral.
Ministar Your starship is to be given a place of honour in the galactic war museum.
Crew No.
Ministar Yes . . . and finally, President Sekurikor has paid, into an undisclosed fund, namely, the "Sam Galactic Good Time Community Chest", the undivulged sum of one million Good Time Coupons.

Sam (*leaping up*) Three of the four things I have always wanted.
Suey What is the florth, Claptain?
Sam I can't tell you . . . you'll . . . say I'm mad.
Alura We won't, we won't.
Lolita What is it?
Sam I think I'm in love
All He's mad.

Speck faints to the floor

Sam No, not quite. Mr Suey, prepare a laser lit supper for two.
Suey Stlaight away, sir.

> *The crew all fade off the set to collect wedding gifts*
>
> *A table is slid into a position upstage* C. *It has a cloth, candle in a bottle and is accompanied by the Luncheonette Ensemble. They are playing a Hungarian romantic melody. The musicians have red roses in their teeth*

Dazzle and Sam dance cheek to cheek across the stage. When in position Sam speaks to the audience

Sam You are about to witness a love bond.
Dazzle One small step for Dazzle.
Sam One giant leap for Galactic.

They moon down to the table and sit misty-eyed holding hands across the table. The music softens

> Waiter.

We hear the sound of Dr Who's "Tardis" landing. A Waiter dressed like Dr Who wrapped in a huge scarf enters

Waiter Yes sir?
Dazzle (*breaking from reverie*) Haven't I seen you somewhere before?
Waiter There is a great deal of unemployment at present, miss.
Dazzle I see.
Waiter Your order, sir?
Sam Two Cupid Stings . . . without cream.
Dazzle (*as if that is reckless*) Oh Sam.
Waiter I'm sorry, sir we've run out of cream. Would you prefer two Cupid Stings without milk, sir?
Sam Fine.
Dazzle Perfect.

> *The Waiter exits*

Sam takes Dazzle's hand across the table and the Hungarian music swells suddenly

Sam Oh Dazzle. I want our love bond to be the purest of the pure.
Dazzle The purest of the pure.
Sam The most untainted of the untaintedest.

Dazzle (*after a pause*) The purest of the pure.

Sam But do you know what we have to do before we can achieve forgiveness of sin?

Dazzle Yes. (*She looks out to the audience*) Sin.

Sam Affirmative.

They rush into an embrace when . . .

The Waiter enters

Waiter Two Cupid Stings without milk, sir.

Sam takes both glasses, hands one to Dazzle; they come forward and raise them

Sam
Dazzle } (*together*) To us.

They interlink arms and drink. Their bodies start to twitch as they go through a kind of comical sensual transformation which culminates when Sam can hold out no longer and sweeps Dazzle into his arms Valentino fashion. They kiss and freeze as, off-stage, the Chorus starts to sing "Space Angel" very quietly

Song 14: Space Angel (Reprise)

Waiter (*out front*) This is what is known as "sinning" and on Procyon it carries a very heavy fine.

Sam produces a money note which he passes over his shoulder to the Waiter without flinching

Thank you, sir. (*He turns to go and stops*) Oh, by the way, they will live happily ever after. Right, Gary?

The Waiter exits

The music increases slightly as the follow spot picks up Gary Gemini coming through the slide door and down to the loving couple. He carries a suitcase labelled "JUST BONDED" which he gives to Sam

Gary Right. Hi there. This *is* Gary Gemini to remind you that Duotronic takes care of *nice* people.

Sam Dazzle, will you join me in Paradise?

Dazzle Oh Sam, it's just like Mummy always said it would be.

Gary (*turning to them*) Sam and Dazzle, to speed you on your honeytrek to that warp factor wonderland beyond the clouds, Duotronic Nuptial Goods is proud to present you with your . . .

The crew come down from the starship with the gifts. They are large, light, beautifully gift-wrapped packages

As Dazzle receives each package she dumps it on Sam; the pile gets heavier and more difficult to manage

Pearl Romeo . . .

Mohammed ... and Juliet ...
Pearl ... slumberspace ...
Mohammed ... bed linen.

They go past and exit R

Gary Your ...
Lolita ... Troilus ...
Paddy ... and Cressida ...
Lolita ... unbreakable ...
Paddy ... tableware.
Gary Your ...
Alura ... Don Juan dual tub ...
Suey ... dishwasher.
Gary And finally your ...
Speck (*nearly in tears at the separation*) ... year's supply of Cupid Stings ...
without milk.

He collapses in tears and staggers off—a broken man

Gary OK. This is Gary Gemini saying thanks for being with us, asking you
not to forget to take the sweet dream pills in your space-pak programme
and reminding you that Duotronic cares.

Gary exits through the slide doors and as his toothy smile fades ...

*We focus on Sam and Dazzle, Sam loaded down with the weight of the gifts,
Dazzle cool. She goes to exit then stops and turns as Sam hasn't moved*

Dazzle Samuel!!
Sam Coming, beloved. (*He moves across the stage and then stops and
addresses out front*) Marriage. The final frontier!

Black-out

Curtain Call (Chorus and principals) to "MAN ABOVE ALL MEN"

Song 15: Man Above All Men (Reprise)

PLAYOUT

As the audience leave we hear the final jingle

Jingle K: Sleep tight with Duotronic Household Goods

CURTAIN

FURNITURE AND PROPERTY LIST

Please see Production Notes for full description of set and props.

BLAST OFF

On stage: Silver frame on cyclorama

Sci-fi doorway R:
Sliding doors
Steps

Starship interior L:
Sunburster door
Computer panel with vision screen
Below computer: shelf with sprays, beauty items, notepad and pen
First aid box. *In it:* plasters, bandages, bottle of tonic, spoon
Tricorder
Control panel at helm. *Behind it:* guns, bombs, etc.
Seats
Silly telescope
4 transporter tubes. *Inside them:* communicators

Off stage: Newsdesk with practical flash camera, chair **(Stage Management)**
Chemistry set **(Speck)**
Huge saw **(Mohammed)**
Medical case with plasters, box of capsules, thermometer, sling, bloodied headband **(Pearl)**
Book **(Suey)**
Space weapon **(Lolita)**
"Irish Lego" box **(Paddy)**
Certificate, digital watch, vests **(Wise Ones)**
Stingray guns **(Bolshies)**
Razor, towel, shaving cream on face **(Paddy)**
Tables, chairs, cloths, candles in bottle, matches, plates of food, silver spacesticks **(Chinese Waiters)**
Blue pills **(Angela** and **Gary)**

Personal: **Angela:** huge glasses
Alura: chewing gum
Crew: choc bars
Paddy: handle
Dazzle: bottle of nail varnish
Mohammed: piece of paper
Speck: pencil behind ear
Waiters: fans

TOUCH DOWN

Set: In starship:
World War II tin helmet
Protective ear headphones
Bottle
Hairnets
Piece of green plastic
Dazzle star concealed upstage

Off stage: Water pistols **(Slimeys)**
Seaweed ropes **(Dazzle)**
Large green syringe **(Swampey)**
Coil of seaweed **(Stage Management)**
Underwater shuttle cock **(Crew)**
Bloodied headband, crutches **(Gary)**
Bikes, Cokes, chains, etc. **(Greasers)**
Communicator **(Sam)**
Motor bike **(Sue Zuki)**
Medical case containing battery-operated mixer (*practical*), bottle of
   Pimple Pulverizer **(Mohammed)**
Communicator **(Speck)**
Computer sphere **(Stage Management)**
Scroll **(Ministar)**
Table with cloth, candle in bottle, 2 chairs **(Luncheonettes)**
Instruments, red roses **(Luncheonette Ensemble)**
2 Cupid Stings **(Waiter)**
Suitcase **(Gary)**
Gift-wrapped packages **(Crew)**

Personal: **Slimebag:** 2 black patches over eyes, hook for right hand
Swampey: hook for left hand
Slimeys: garlands or leis (*concealed*)
Dazzle: notebook, pencil
Greasers: black freckles
Sue Zuki: American Express card
Vic: 2 cards in pocket
Sam: money

LIGHTING PLOT

Property fittings required: nil

Three playing areas: starship interior, central main playing area, sci-fi doorway

BLAST OFF

To open: Follow spot on **Gary**

Cue 1	As **Gary** sweeps down to central playing area *Bring up general lighting*	(Page 1)
Cue 2	**Gary** exits L *Centre spot on* **Angela**	(Page 2)
Cue 3	As **Sekurikor** and **Wise Ones** enter *Change to gold lighting*	(Page 2)
Cue 4	As **Sam** appears at door L *Follow spot on him*	(Page 3)
Cue 5	**Wise ones** and **Sekurikor** fade from set *Narrow light down to* **Sam** *and* **Crew**	(Page 6)
Cue 6	**Crew** move into position for Song 2 *Increase lighting* C	(Page 6)
Cue 7	**Crew** stride across on to starship interior *Cross-fade to lighting on starship*	(Page 7)
Cue 8	**Suey:** "Audio-visual on." *Fade lights slightly; bring up light behind vision screen*	(Page 9)
Cue 9	**Sam:** 'Scanner off." *Fade light on vision screen and return to previous lighting on starship*	(Page 9)
Cue 10	**Alura:** "... here she comes." *Fade lighting on starship slightly*	(Page 10)
Cue 11	**Sam:** Searchlight probe on." *Follow spot on* **Dazzle** *as she enters*	(Page 11)
Cue 12	During Song 3 *Lighting on central playing area*	(Page 11)
Cue 13	**Sam** leads **Dazzle** to starship interior *Cross-fade to starship*	(Page 12)
Cue 14	**Dazzle:** "... at those stars." *Light narrows, or follow spot on* **Dazzle** *and* **Sam**	(Page 12)

Cue 15	**Crew** descend on central playing area *Cross-fade to central playing area*	(Page 13)
Cue 16	At end of Song 4 *Cross-fade to starship*	(Page 15)
Cue 17	**Mohammed:** "Hold on everybody." *Lights flicker up and down*	(Page 16)
Cue 18	**Pearl:** "Video screen activating, sir." *Repeat Cue 8*	(Page 16)
Cue 19	**Big Olga:** "... very angry. Oi!" *Fade light on vision screen*	(Page 16)
Cue 20	**Sam:** "Energize." *Lights oscillate, then black-out; when ready, bring up lighting* R	(Page 18)
Cue 21	As **Bolshies** enter *Red lighting*	(Page 18)
Cue 22	**Suey:** "Energizing now, sir." *Dip lights briefly*	(Page 21)
Cue 23	**Big Olga:** "No." Phaser is fired *Explosion; flicker lights*	(Page 22)
Cue 24	**Suey:** "Bleaming up, Claptain." *Fade lights; when ready, bring up lighting on starship*	(Page 23)
Cue 25	**Pearl:** "... time-slip time." *Fade lights slowly; focus on girls*	(Page 24)
Cue 26	At end of Song 6 *After a moment, return to previous lighting*	(Page 25)
Cue 27	As **Gary** and **Angela** enter *Light on them; as they speak, fade lighting on Crew*	(Page 28)
Cue 28	**Angela** and **Gary** go into a clinch again *Fade lights; bring up house lights*	(Page 29)

TOUCH DOWN

To open: Black-out

Cue 29	After Jingle 7 *Snap up lighting on* **Gary** *and* **Angela**	(Page 30)
Cue 30	**Crew** enter *Increase lighting*	(Page 30)
Cue 31	They all scream *Lights dip*	(Page 30)
Cue 32	**Pearl:** "We're under attack." *Flicker lights*	(Page 30)
Cue 33	**Sam:** "Slimebag the Haemorrhage." *Flood main playing area with green light; fade lighting on starship*	(Page 31)

Cue 34	As **Dazzle** raises star *Follow spot on it*	(Page 35)
Cue 35	**Dazzle** pretends to throw star *Dim lights; track supposed path with follow spot*	(Page 35)
Cue 36	**Crew** pull out invisible plug *Lights flash—continue*	(Page 36)
Cue 37	When ready *Steady lights on starship*	(Page 36)
Cue 38	**Suey:** "Audio on." *Repeat Cue 8*	(Page 36)
Cue 39	**Lolita:** "And save all humanity." *Repeat Cue 9*	(Page 37)
Cue 40	**Dazzle:** ". . . the pig's committed." *Flash lights*	(Page 39)
Cue 41	**Gary** faints *Black-out*	(Page 39)
Cue 42	When ready *Bring up lighting on central playing area*	(Page 39)
Cue 43	**Vic:** ". . . Magic Circle or sunnink." *Dim down lights to cover entrance of **Mohammed**, **Pearl**, etc.* *Return to previous lighting when ready*	(Page 44)
Cue 44	As **Sue Zuki** jumps up and down *Momentary Black-out*	(Page 45)
Cue 45	**Greasers:** "Right." *Cross-fade to starship*	(Page 48)
Cue 46	At end of Song 13 *Lights change slightly*	(Page 49)
Cue 47	**Crew** enter central playing area *Cross-fade to central playing area*	(Page 50)
Cue 48	**Sekurikor:** ". . . in the computer sphere." *Follow spot on star*	(Page 51)
Cue 49	As **Speck** places star on top of sphere *Sphere pulses*	(Page 51)
Cue 50	**Sekurikor:** "Of course." *Dim lights; follow spot on Ministar*	(Page 51)
Cue 51	**Ministar:** ". . . Good Time Coupons." *Fade follow spot*	(Page 51)
Cue 52	As **Gary** comes in through slide door *Follow spot on him*	(Page 53)
Cue 53	**Gary** exits *Cut follow spot; focus on **Sam** and **Dazzle***	(Page 54)

Cue 54   **Sam:** "The final frontier!"   (Page 54)
            Black-out

Cue 55   When ready   (Page 54)
            Lights up for Song 15 and curtain calls

EFFECTS PLOT

BLAST OFF

Cue 1   **Gary:** "... music of the future."   (Page 1)
Jingle A

Cue 2   **Angela:** "... Duotronic Household Goods."   (Page 1)
Jingle B

Cue 3   **Gary** gives title of song   (Page 1)
Short piece of radiophonic music with words dubbed on

Cue 4   Spot centres on **Angela**   (Page 2)
Jingle D

Cue 5   **Sekurikor:** "... the names be named."   (Page 3)
Jingle E

Cue 6   **Lolita:** "I fire 'em!"   (Page 5)
Terrible racket off L

Cue 7   **Gary:** "... from Duotronic Household Goods."   (Page 8)
Jingle F

Cue 8   **Crew** bite choc bars   (Page 8)
Star Trek music

Cue 9   **Suey:** "Audio-visual on."   (Page 9)
Humming sound for a few seconds

Cue 10   **Paddy** (*off*): "Right you are, sir."   (Page 10)
Champagne cork pops, off

Cue 11   **Paddy:** "... Duotronic Household Goods."   (Page 21)
Jingle G

Cue 12   **Big Olga:** "No."   (Page 21)
Phaser is fired—explosion

Cue 13   As house lights come up   (Page 29)
Jingle H

TOUCH DOWN

Cue 14   As house lights go down   (Page 30)
Jingle I

Cue 15   **Crew** adopt freeze positions   (Page 30)
Jingle J

Cue 16   **Pearl:** "We're under attack."   (Page 30)
Alert sounds

MADE AND PRINTED IN GREAT BRITAIN BY
LATIMER TREND & COMPANY LTD PLYMOUTH

MADE IN ENGLAND